BIZ
BLOG
MARKETING

BIZ
BLOG
MARKETING

SECRETS OF BUSINESS BLOG MARKETING FOR SMALL BUSINESS

DOUG WILLIAMS

PRODUCED AND PUBLISHED BY:
DOUG WILLIAMS AND ASSOCIATES, LLC
VANCOUVER, WA

For information and ordering please contact:
Doug Williams and Associates, LLC
7414 NE Hazel Dell Avenue Suite C
Vancouver, WA 98665
Tel: (800) 393-7740

First Edition
2008   01
Printed in the United States of America

Library of Congress Control Number: 2007910390
Publisher: Doug Williams and Associates, LLC
Vancouver, Washington

ISBN-10   0-9801307-0-0
ISBN-13   978-0-9801307-0-6

Biz Blog Marketing

Table of Contents

Chapter 4 Marketing and Internet Marketing 63

Chapter 8 Blog Writing 130

Legal Stuff

Introduction

Business blogs are sweeping the business community. Find out what they are, how they work and what they can do for your business. Incorporate blogging into your business marketing plans has many advantages.

Blog marketing can increase exposure, generate buzz, and create a global message to which individual customers can respond. Blog marketing is also a powerful search engine optimization tool which can be used to dramatically improve website rankings.

You will be able to get business from new markets, be viewed as an expert in your field and be able to promote your company website with the search engines. Our system is focused on sales, lead generation, and branding goals for your company.

Biz Blog Marketing is the complete Book that you need to take advantage of business blogging. In addition to this Book, Doug Williams and Associates offers consulting, blog planning and blogging websites. We also put on workshops and training for management teams.

This book has been written in a blogging format. This means that most (not all) were written in a short concise format that is quick and easy to read. Each chapter is made up of multiple topics. Each topic is about 250 words long, in the same way that blog postings should be written.

In this book, you will learn:

1. How blog marketing works
2. How to write a blog posting
3. How commenting on other people's blogs will help you
4. The secrets of SEO to promote your website and blog
5. How to create and optimize video blogs
6. Sample blogging plans with specific strategies and tactics for many different businesses in many industries

About the Author Doug Williams

Doug Williams is the founder and president of Doug Williams and Associates (DWA), a business consulting and Internet marketing firm located in Vancouver, Washington. Since 2002 DWA has helped owners grow their businesses and their bottom line thru business coaching, marketing strategies, blog marketing, search engine optimization, web design and web programming solutions.

A results oriented business consultant, Doug is experienced in designing and implementing strategic plans and business systems. His key strength is the ability to originate and implement change. Doug has expertise in marketing, financial, operations and general management in companies experiencing rapid change in both high growth and start-up situations. He has served on the Board of Directors for multiple companies.

Prior to becoming a consultant, Doug spent 26 years in management, 22 of these years in senior management positions across a wide range of industries. During this time, he defined and put in place many key business systems and improvement strategies to create profitable operations.

Doug has an MBA from Pepperdine University and an undergraduate degree in Biology and Chemistry from CSU Northridge.

For more information, visit www.DougWilliams.com

Chapter 1 What is a Blog?

So what is a Blog anyway? Recently, there has been a great deal of talk about blogs. Blogs can be personal or business related. Business blogs or corporate blogs are one of the hottest growth areas for blogs and is opening new markets for business. Blogs allow anyone to quickly post text and images to the Web without any special technical knowledge. This opens the web up to more publishing and distribution of information.

What is it?
Blog is short for weblog. A blog is a regularly updated journal published on the web. Wouldn't it be nice if the readers of a website could leave comments, about a specific article? With blogs, they can! Posting comments is one of the best features of blogs. Blogs generally represent the personality of the author or the Web site.

Some blogs are intended for a small audience; others have a readership of national newspapers. On a blog, the content consists of articles — also sometimes called "posts" or "entries."

A Blog is a Web site that contains dated entries in reverse chronological order (most recent first) about a particular topic. A blog has unfiltered content — some feel that the second somebody filters or edits the author it's no longer a blog.

Blogs are influential, personal, or both, and they reflect as many topics and opinions as there are people writing them. Many blogs focus on a particular topic, such as web design, politics, sports, or mobile technology. Some are more eclectic, presenting links to all manner of other sites. And others are more like personal journals, presenting the author's daily life and thoughts.

Blogs represent one of the defining differences of web 2.0 or the second generation Internet.

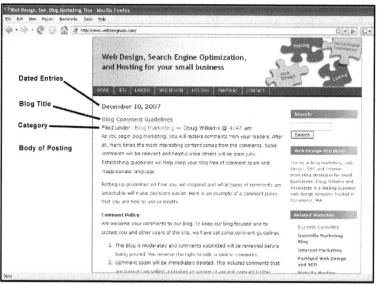

Screenshot of Author's blog showing the major elements that makes up a blog. www.webdesignseo.com

"The evidence that things are changing fast can be seen in the dramatic increase in the influence of blogging."- Adam Rickitt

The Origins and History of Blogs

So when did blogging begin? Although blogs are a recent invention, the idea is not new. Blogs evolved from online diaries that people kept from the earliest days of the Internet. Blogs as we think of them today are a combination of a personal journal, a message board and a news site. Let's look at the milestones of blogging.

1994 – It is uncertain who started the very first blog. Justin Hall is credited by some to be the "founding father" of blogging for starting his "Proto-Blog" in December 1994 while still a student at Swarthmore College. Justin maintained this online journaling for 11 years.

1997 Jorn Barger first used the term "web log" to describe a simple website where people post interesting links that they found while surfing the net.

1998 Open Diary launched their website which would grow to thousands. Open Diary is credited with adding the ability for readers to make comments

1999 Peter Merholz breaks weblog apart into "We Blog." This was quickly adopted and shortened to blog. LiveJournal and Blogger.com were launched as the first hosted blog tools.

2002 Heather Armstrong is fired for discussing her job in her personal blog which was named "Dooce." Dooced becomes the term that means "Fired for blogging."

2004 Merriam-Webster the prominent dictionary publisher announced that "Blog" was the word of the year. 2004 marked a turning point where blogging became adopted into everyday life.

By the end of 2007 there were over 110 million blogs being tracked. Millions of people look to blogs as their source for information, news or just a good laugh.

RSS (Real Simple Syndication)

RSS can stand for Real Simple Syndication or Rich Site Summary. Either way, RSS is an important technology that makes your blog postings available to be read across the Internet. RSS is what makes News articles available for searches almost immediately after they are posted.

RSS are simple text files that are submitted to feed directories. These allow subscribers and search engines to see content within a very short time.

Blogs generate a behind-the-scenes text code in a language called XML. This code, usually referred to as a "feed" (as in "news feed"), makes it possible for readers to "subscribe" to the content that is created on a particular blog. This way the content comes to you instead of you going to it.

Your blog automatically notifies popular Update Services that you've updated your blog. In turn, update services process the ping and updates their proprietary indices with your update. Your blog has been set-up to notify more than 30 different update services each time you make a change. It can take as little as only a few hours to appear in search engine results.

RSS enables users to subscribe to data feeds easily, which lets them control the rate and amount of information coming to them online. They receive your updates by either email or via blog feed. Blog reader programs typically have the option to show the full article or just a summary (or the beginning) to syndication feeds. Readers can then come to your site to read the whole article.

How RSS Makes Your Blog Work

RSS is at the heart of what makes a blog work. Remember a blog is a special website that allows easy web publishing with a content management system (CMS) and notifies the web each time a new article is posted (RSS). So how does this work?

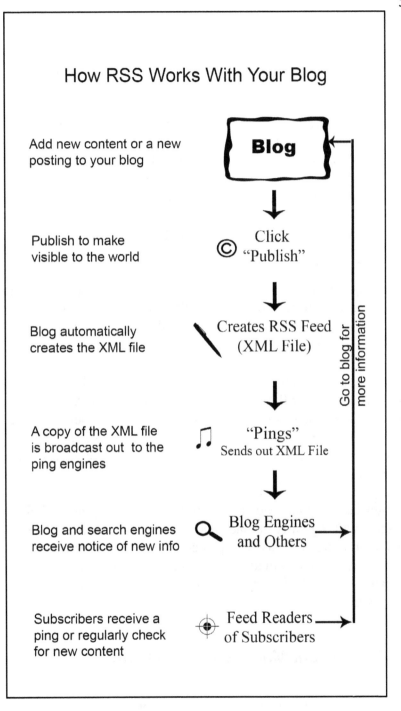

How RSS Works With Your Blog

Add new content or a new posting to your blog

Blog

Publish to make visible to the world

© Click "Publish"

Blog automatically creates the XML file

Creates RSS Feed (XML File)

A copy of the XML file is broadcast out to the ping engines

"Pings" Sends out XML File

Go to blog for more information

Blog and search engines receive notice of new info

Blog Engines and Others

Subscribers receive a ping or regularly check for new content

Feed Readers of Subscribers

Once you create a new article or posting, you are able to make this public by publishing what you wrote. When you publish, three things happen.

1. What you wrote immediately becomes visible to your blog visitors.
2. Your blog creates an RSS-XML file that is easily read by search engines and blog engines. These XML files are really a simple text file called a feed.
3. A ping is sent out to notify that you have something new on your blog. This invites blog engines and subscribers to look at your new content.

The blog ping that is sent out is a small XML file that contains the blog title, a brief description and a link to where the new content can be found. This ping is received by the major services which notifies search engines you now have new content.

The blog and search engines will either display the XML feeds they received or will send their own spiders back to retrieve more information. The results are, that what you write is being indexed and available on the Internet within minutes of being published. This is a similar process to the way news stories are released to the Internet.

Subscribers to your feed can either be notified by ping or their feed readers will regularly go back and check your RSS-XML files to see if anything new has been posted. When the reader finds updates, it makes them available to the recipient. The readers usually display the information from the XML files with a link to the content.

CMS (Content Management System)

CMS or Content Management System is software that provides a method of managing your website. They provide the features required to create and maintain a blog, and can make publishing on the Internet as simple as writing an article.

All blogs run on some type of CMS. A content management system is a web-based application connected to a database that allows writers to create and update blog content without having to know HTML (Hypertext Markup Language) or any other programming language.

CMS allows writers with no special web technical knowledge to write and format their thoughts and publish to the web in a few minutes. Blog writers can create their postings as easily as typing a letter and then publishing with a single push of a button.

Using CMS, blog content can be created using a WYSIWYG (What You See Is What You Get) web page editor. When a blog posting needs to be altered in some way, you just open up the blog posting, make the changes, and upload the new file. Blogs are just another way of using browser-based tools for creating, managing and publishing your thoughts, opinions, or activities directly to the web. The technology behind blogs is basic CMS functionality that originated back in the mid '90s.

Using CMS, writers can format their work; add photos and images just like they would in their favorite word processing program. These changes are made directly on the web server from any computer that has web access.

RSS Feed Readers

In the blogging world, a "feed reader" or feed aggregator is a software application that collects web content such as news headlines, blogs, podcasts, and vlogs into a single location for easy viewing.

Feeds are a free, quick and efficient way to read new web content, news and blogs. A web feed is a document (often XML-based) which contains content items with web links to longer versions. News websites and blogs are common sources for web feeds.

"Publishing a feed" and "syndication" are two of the more common terms used to describe making available a feed from an information source, such as a blog. The two main web feed formats are RSS and Atom.

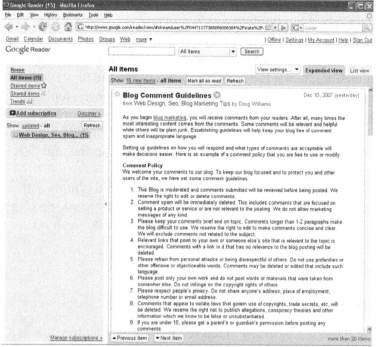

Google Reader (http://www.google.com/reader/) is one of the popular feed readers in use today

Like syndicated print newspaper features or broadcast programs, web feed contents may be shared and republished by other websites. This is why one popular definition of RSS is Really Simple Syndication. Syndication is undoubtedly the heartbeat of the web 2.0 movement.

Usually feeds are subscribed to directly by users with aggregators or feed readers, which combine the content of multiple web feeds to be displayed on a single screen or series of screens. Some modern web browsers incorporate aggregator features.

Feed readers allow you to customize, organize, search and categorize articles. There are a number of different types of readers: web-based, desktop, Outlook based, etc... These feed aggregators act as your agent, collecting and presenting to you your own customized online newspaper.

Popular web based feed readers include: NewzCrawler, FeedDemon, Bloglines, Google Reader, NewsGator and Blog Navigator.

Types of Blogging Software

Blogging software comes in both hosted and self-hosted types. Hosted blogs are hosted by the blog service and are easier for creating a personal blog. Self-hosted blogs require downloading software and is better for business blogging because it gives the control for branding and marketing.

Hosted Blogs: A user simply needs to sign up, set-up a blog account and start blogging. These blogs are hosted on a central server and are very easy for the novice to get going quickly. All software updates and database maintenance is done by the provider. This type of hosting is required with services such as Blogger or TypePad and optional with services such as WordPress.

The main disadvantage of a hosted solution is the limitations. You are limited to having your blog on their domain. You are limited on the themed looks that are available and you are limited on how you can optimize your blog for search engines. This is fine for a personal blog, but not good for business blogging.

Self-Hosted: This is very much like setting up a website. Here a domain name is purchased, a hosting account is set-up, the blog software is downloaded, a database is set-up and the blog is configured. Which blog platforms can be self hosted? These include WordPress, Textpattern and Movable Type.

The advantage of a self-hosted blog is you get maximum benefits of control, flexibility and customization. Business blog marketing will usually use self-hosted blogs so they can control everything about the look and operation of the blog. They can customize the templates, incorporate plug-ins and optimize their blog for the search engines.

Blogging Platforms

Hosted   **Vs.**   **Self Hosted**

They host   *You host*

Easier   **More Control**

Blogger   Moveable Type

TypePad   Textpattern

WordPress.com   Wordpress.org

Choosing Blogging Software

Which business blogging software should you use? In a quick search of the Internet we came up with over 60 possible choices. Four of the most popular blogging platforms are Blogger, Movable Type, TypePad and WordPress.

1. **Blogger** is the most popular hosted solution. Owned by Google and free to use, it is full featured and must be hosted from their central server. This makes it easy to sign up for and maintain. It is not our choice for business blogging because of limited customization options. It still remains an excellent choice for personal blogs.

2. **Movable Type** was released in 2001 and dominated the blogging market from 2002-2004. Owned by Six Apart, Movable Type is free for personal use and commercial licenses range from $200-$800. This must be self-hosted. This is full featured blogging software, but it is built on older technologies. It can slow down over time with a large number of blog entries. A good choice for business blogging, just not our top choice.

3. **TypePad** is owned by Six Apart and was released in 2003. TypePad is only offered as a hosted blogging solution. Pricing packages range from $4.95 to $29.95 per month. TypePad has many tools and features and allows for the addition of photo albums. But in the end, it is still a hosted solution and not customizable enough to meet the needs of business blogging.

4. **WordPress** started in 2003 and is an Open Source project. This means there are hundreds of developers worldwide working on developments, plug-ins and improvements and it is free. Available in hosted and self-hosted versions. For business blogging, we recommend the self-hosted version. Because it is completely customizable, it is our top choice for business blogging.

Comparison: Blogger vs. Wordpress.org

For business blog marketing should you use Blogger, the Google hosted product or Wordpress.org? Blogger and Wordpress.org are the two leading blogging platforms in use today for blogging.

Over and over I talk with bloggers that started with Blogger because it is free and easy to set-up. Then they realize the limitations and need to convert to the self-hosted version of WordPress. The Wordpress.org product in our opinion is a much better product for business applications because it can be customized to give better blog marketing results.

Wordpress.org should not be confused with Wordpress.com which is a hosted version similar to Blogger.

Blogger
Blogger is owned by Google and it is free. It is an excellent tool for the beginner. Hosting is done on blogspot.com.

Advantages
1. It is free.
2. Set-up is easy and quick. No coding knowledge required.
3. Pre-installed themes, templates, plugins and widgets.
4. Software is updated automatically for you.
5. Built-in spam controls.

Disadvantages
1. Limited control and limited ability to customize.
2. Design choices limited; making it difficult to achieve a distinct look.
3. Code produced is not valid W3C valid code.
4. "No Follow" cannot be removed from comments.
5. Lacks categories to organize posts. Uses labels instead.

Wordpress.org
Wordpress.org is the free open source blogging platform that you download and run on your own hosting account.

Advantages
1. You can completely control and customize blog functionality.
2. Ability to organize posts by category.
3. WordPress is built following W3C code standards.
4. Large library of plug-ins available to add functionality.
5. Multiple user security levels.

Disadvantages
1. Set-up and customization is more complex.
2. Longer learning curve because of available options.
3. Requires setting up a hosting account.
4. Requires a separate domain name.
5. Tech support is available thru forums and wikis.

Our recommendation is strongly for Wordpress.org. Hundreds of independent developers regularly produce new plug-ins and customizations making this the most versatile and best performing blogging platform available. For the beginning Blogger, is easier and quicker to set-up and is a better choice for the "tech-challenged."

Blog Search Engines

Understanding traffic sources is an important element in blog marketing. Blog traffic can come from direct sources, RSS feeds, from other referral sources or from blog search engines.

In terms of blog search engines, Google and Technorati are the largest players. There are quite a number of other blog search engines and directories in use today. Directories are a great place to submit your blog and receive a valued link which will help promote your blog.

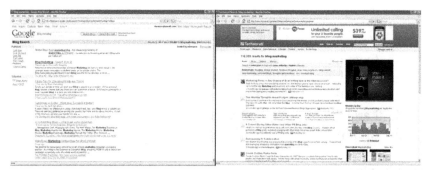

Google Blog Search and Technorati are two of the most popular blog search engines in use today. These are screenshots of the search pages for each.

Where will your blog traffic come from? For me, I receive about 40% from search engines and 60% from all other sources (direct and referrals).

The following resource list is a great list to research and can be valued sources of traffic for your blog. This is a current resource list sorted by alphabetical order.

Name	URL	Description
Amatomu	http://www.amatomu.com/	South African Blog Search engine
Blog Catalog	http://www.blogcatalog.com/	Blog Directory
Blog Pulse	http://www.blogpulse.com/	Blog Search Engine and Statistics
Blog Rate Directory	http://www.blogratedirectory.com/	Blog Directory and Blog Rating site
Blogdigger	http://www.blogdigger.com/	Small search engine
Bloggernity	http://www.bloggernity.com/	Bog search engine and directory
Bloghop	http://www.bloghop.com/search.htm	Small search engine

Bloghub	http://www.bloghub.com/	Blog Directory
Bloglines	http://www.bloglines.com/	Search and aggregate RSS feeds
Blogrunner	http://www.blogrunner.com/	Blog search engine
BlogScope	http://www.blogscope.net/	Blog analysis and visualization tool
Blogsearchengine	http://www.blogsearchengine.com/	Blog search engine
Blogstreet	http://www.blogstreet.com/search.html	Metasearch
Eaton Web	http://portal.eatonweb.com/	Blog Directory
Google Blog Search	http://blogsearch.google.com/	Blog search engine
Ice Rocket	http://www.icerocket.com/	Blog / Internet Search Engine
Read A Blog	http://www.readablog.com/	Blog Search Engine
Sphere	http://www.sphere.com/	Blog Search Engine
Technorati	http://www.technorati.com/	Blog search engine and listings

Why Blogs Are Better Than Websites

1. **Blogs are active and websites are passive**. Blogs broadcast their content out to the web via RSS every time there is something new. Websites on the other hand wait to be discovered by search engine spiders. It's like the difference between fishing and hunting. You can sit and wait for fish or you can actively hunt and pursue.
2. **Blogs are faster**. Posting and syndication is almost instantaneous. Technorati and other blog search engines index and list your postings within minutes after you publish.
3. **Blogs build a readership**. It is easy for visitors to subscribe to a blog so they can view new postings as soon as they happen. Blogs encourage repeat visits with content being delivered to your favorite reader or delivery by email.

Compare this to bookmarking a website which depends on the visitor to come back.

4. **Blogs have newer fresher content**. By their nature, blogs have regular fresh content and they are more up to date. Blogs tend to deal with breaking events and technology insights.

5. **Blogs invite participation and interaction**. Blog conversations are encouraged providing multiple viewpoints and discussions. Comments can be made easily from each page.

6. **Blogs make it personal**. Blog writing is more informal and conversational. It allows the writer's personality to make it more alive and interesting. Websites on the other hand are more formal and tend to be written in marketing speak.

7. **Blogs are easier**. You don't need to understand HTML to publish your thoughts and opinions. The content management systems on blogs allow you to type, format and add pictures as easily as you can in a word processing program.

8. **Blogs allow scheduling**. You can pre-write your postings and schedule them to appear at a given time and on a given day. This means you can work ahead and have your postings appear even when you are on vacation. Working ahead may make it harder to talk about current happenings, but it sure is convenient.

"The ability to express an idea is well nigh as important as the idea itself." - Bernard M. Baruch

Chapter 2 About Business Blog Marketing

Blog marketing uses blogs to publicize or advertise a website or business. Business blog marketing is simply marketing your business using a blog. About 70% of all businesses have a website of some sort today: this is website marketing. Less than 10% of businesses today are currently using blogs to promote their business: this is business blog marketing. Blog marketing is starting to become commonplace as companies start to use the Internet for publicity.

Blogs are a communication tool used to provide an engaging online experience for your customers. Business Blog Marketing is a strategy used for marketing, visibility and branding. It is also effective to help generate leads, increase sales, improve communications and promote your brand online. A blog makes your business visible. Blogs open up new markets.

Blog marketing builds a following of customers and prospects that are interested in your company's products and services. The goal is to create a following of readers who will give feedback and comments to what you have to offer or things you plan on offering. Blog Marketing is about consistent posting of valuable information to your readers on an ongoing basis.

Effective marketing is a two way communication. Trade shows and workshops are examples of marketing that allows two way communications. Surveys are used to understand what your customers are thinking. Blogs allow a conversational type relationship with your customer that allows feedback.

Business blog marketing allows your marketing to talk directly to customers. A business blog is a communication tool that allows your business to reach a new audience by writing in a conversational way and showing the human and personal side of the business.

"At its best, blogging is all about change. The format suits writers who want to move fast." - Naomi Darvell

Business Blogging is Different

Business blogging is different than personal blogging. A business blog is an online business and marketing tool. It is a blog with a purpose, with a focus and one to get measurable results from. Business blogs can interact with a target market on a more personal level than other business marketing methods.

A personal blog is really an online diary or journal that gives the writer a chance to share online experiences, opinions and to generate new ideas. A personal blog can go wherever the writer wants.

A business blog is meant to promote, establish a relationship with readers and potential customers, to build anticipation and to generate a buzz. They separate you and your company from the pack and help to build both trust and your reputation within your business' targeted area.

Business blogging requires a different tone and approach. It is about taking that one extra step. People prefer to do business with people that they know and trust. You have to be aware of what you are saying and what image you are giving. It means being focused on your customer.

Business blogging causes you to think of PR implications for every post. You are representing your business, not just your personal opinions. Opinions written on a Business blog are taken as company positions much more than that of one employee's particular opinion on his/her personal blog.

Blogging takes discipline and time commitment. The benefits of blogging for businesses of all sizes are sufficiently great to motivate almost any business to take up the practice of blogging.

Why Businesses Blog

Businesses are turning to blogging as a marketing tool. Why? Because it gets results and gets results faster than traditional Internet marketing. Business blogging is a way to boost their online brand, to increase their importance with the search engines, to reach new potential clients, to communicate with current customers and to publicize information about their company.

Blogs are the new marketing tool that we can add to our bag of traditional marketing strategies. Blogs allow us to reach our targeted marketing niche. In the past few years, blogging has moved from the early adopters to the mainstream in business.

Blogs are now the most trusted media source for useful information according to a Blogads survey of over 35,000 readers. Value was compared against newspaper, radio, television, direct mail and magazines. It is estimated that in the US 27% of the people read blogs on a regular basis.

Blogs are powerful influencers. "More than half (52%) of Europeans polled said that they were more likely to purchase a product if they had read positive comments from private individuals on the internet." This is according to a Hotwire Ipsos MORI survey.

Blogs distribute information very quickly and efficiently.

Because blog feeds are similar to news feeds, information spreads very quickly. Blogs are a great place to kick-start marketing of new products and services.

So what do businesses expect from their blogging efforts?
1. Competitive differentiation
2. Brand building
3. Improve search engine rankings
4. Increase targeted website traffic
5. Direct communications
6. Connect with new customers
7. Positioned as an expert
8. Media and public relations
9. Relational Marketing

"What do I think about when I strike out? I think about hitting home runs". -Babe Ruth

When A Business Should NOT Blog

Blogging is not for everyone. There are businesses that shouldn't be blogging. There are people within a business that shouldn't be writing. There are topics that should never be part of the business's weblog.

Businesses that shouldn't blog

Companies who are unwilling to commit the time and resources to regular blog postings shouldn't even start up a blog. A blog started and abandoned can do more harm than good.

Some companies are heavily government-regulated such as those selling Securities. All of their public communications must go through rigorous review by legal teams. Companies working on military technology could also prove to be a life-and-death issue should any unfortunate leaks of information occur.

People who shouldn't blog

Companies should carefully select their spokesmen. They should stay away from people who are terrible writers, those in sensitive positions and those that lack the judgment on what they can and should be writing about.

Some people lack any form of coherent writing skills. Keep these types of people far away from your company blog. Some executives may not be comfortable publicly expressing their views. Others have difficulty writing in such an informal style.

Topics to Avoid

Finally, there are specific topics that I believe you shouldn't blog about. These are things that are confidential or at least should be. These include blogging about personnel issues, company or trade secrets, legal suits that your company may be involved in, sensitive financial information and individual medical information.

Have a strong political view? This should stay far, far away from any sort of business blog.

Business Blog Marketing Opens New Markets

If you have a business, you need a blog! Business blog marketing opens up new market channels to your business. According to Technorati there are over 100 million blogs. So is anyone reading these? Absolutely!

Out of the 100 most popular websites, 22 were blogs. This is up from 12 just six months ago. Young adults 18-24 read blogs three times more frequently than older adults. If your market is made up of this age demographic, blogging is a very effective way to reach this segment.

Why should a business set up a corporate blog? Here are 10 reasons:
1. Reach new market demographics than traditional marketing.
2. Relatively low cost and quick to get up and running.
3. Blogs are simple to use and with RSS feeds are effective in reaching large numbers of people.
4. Blogging is branding. Regular posts reach your market segment and make them aware of your products and services.

5. Blogs convey authority. You will quickly be viewed as an expert and a market leader by readers.
6. Search engines love blogs with their regular growth in content and natural link rich format.
7. Blog marketing is also a powerful search engine optimization tool which can be used to dramatically improve website rankings.
8. Information is broadcast at an amazing rate and picked up quickly by the search engines.
9. Feedback can be almost immediate and businesses can find out right away what people think of their company, products and ideas.
10. Add a human face to your company and create a corporate personality.

Blogging Boosts eCommerce Sales

Blogging and eCommerce stores are a natural combination. Most eCommerce stores advertise with a pay-per-click campaign. Most stores lack enough content to satisfy the search engines. On-site blogs are a natural solution in that they supply tons of fresh content.

You need your website as your sales tool, but use a blog to drive traffic to your store.

How will a blog help your store?

1. **Keywords**: Blogs give keyword targeted content and the chance to add in popular keywords related to products and services.

2. **Content:** Focus on content that is interesting to your targeted customer without being promotional. People come to a blog to read interesting stuff. Good ideas for content would be tutorials, tips and project ideas.

3. **Linking:** Using your keywords in the link text and then deep link within your website. Blogs help businesses establish more links to their websites.

4. **Expert Status**: Writing and posting regularly brand your company as the expert or thought leader in the field. People prefer to buy from the experts in a particular market.

Usually blog posts will be listed in the blog search engines in under an hour. Search engines will start displaying them in 1-2 days. Google seems to pick up blog postings the quickest, but you will see rankings improve across all search engines.

Blogging can reduce or eliminate your PPC costs by increasing your rankings in the organic search results. Buyers tend to trust the natural or organic rankings more, you will build a readership and these people will buy from you.

Blog Marketing Ethics

Marketing is targeted at changing the way people act and think. Blog marketing is a powerful new medium. With this power comes an ethical responsibility. Developing an ethics statement for a business blog marketing program is especially important when several people are involved.

This helps avoid ethical misconduct which could damage both image and reputation. It acts as a training tool for internal staff. It promotes open and honest communication and builds up a positive business reputation.

Looking for ideas on what to include? WOMMA, the Word of Mouth Marketing Association, has published a list of ethical guidelines that they encourage businesses to adopt. http://www.womma.org/blogger/

What are considered unethical blogging practices?

1. **Stealth campaigns**: Paid employees or contractors will promote products without disclosing their relationship to the company. The idea is to create an artificial grass roots campaign (Astroturfing). The US Federal Trade Commission has issued an opinion against this practice.

2. **Shilling:** Paying bloggers to post positive comments and recommendations about a product or service. Here bloggers are not free to form their own opinions. This is like hiring actors to rave about a product without disclosing that they are being paid.

3. **Infiltration:** This involves participating in forums or blogs using a fake identity. Then attempt to influence or sway opinions on products and brands. The goal is to confuse or mislead consumers as to identity.

4. **Comment Spam**: Submitting linked blog comments with the intent to try and raise their own websites' search engine rankings. This is usually done with automatic software that posts random comments that promote commercial services.

Businesses involved in blog marketing need to consider the ethics in their own marketing campaign and how this relates to the company's core values.

"A man is truly ethical only when he obeys the compulsion to help all life which he is able to assist, and shrinks from injuring anything that lives." - Albert Schweitzer

Should You Advertise on Your Blog?

This has been a controversial issue and the subject of much debate around the blogosphere. Some oppose all commercial advertising and others use blogging as a way of earning their living. This really comes down to what is the purpose of your blog?

If your objective is to brand your business as an authoritative expert in your industry and image is very important, then you probably will not add advertising to your blog. If your objective is to earn a living from your blog then adding advertising makes a lot of sense.

Pro: You should advertise if the primary objective is to earn income from your blog. The amount of advertising will be based on what your secondary objectives are. The more advertising on your blog, the more ways you are splitting up the attention of your visitor.

There are a number of advertising networks that allow blog owners to earn income. Google Adsense is one of the most popular. Advertising on blogs can range from a few discreet text ads to a garish mess of animated flashing banner ads all striving to get attention.

Con: If your business blogging objectives are about branding and positioning yourself (or your company) as the authoritative expert, then advertising interferes with this. Your goal is to keep your visitor focused on what you have to say. If you elect to allow a minimal amount of ads, are you prepared to allow your direct competitors to advertise on your blog?

The decision to advertise should be based on a balance between business image and income goals that you need from your blog. It is all about the results you need and your blogging goals.

The Art of Promoting…

Marketing blogging is the art of promoting your business with a blog. Blogs are a bigger power-house than most even realize. Blogs seem to be the magazine of the future and have become a leading presence on the Internet. Blog marketing has also become one of the best ways to learn and transmit industry news.

Business blogging has become a merger between social media and marketing. A big part of this blogging is the activity of finding, sharing and recommending products, services, events and experiences to like-minded people. At the heart of social media is the ability of individuals to interact with other people so that they feel involved and part of a community.

A Business Blog is like setting up a booth in the biggest trade show on earth… everyday. Blog marketing should be a part of a company's web site marketing strategy. Companies engaging in business blogging have a definite advantage over their competitors because they reach out to the Blogosphere. Marketing possibilities are just around the corner with the ability to reach new markets and new customers.

Two important characteristics of blogs are that they are written by someone who is knowledgeable and passionate about their subject and they are written in an everyday voice. What is being said is not being filtered and re-written by the marketing, legal and PR departments. This gives blogs an "honesty" that is missing in traditional business communications.

When it comes down to it, blogging can be a great tool to promote your business if used correctly. Remember, the blogging world is immense, so if you are ready to sit down and start a blog, make sure to design a strategy of how to market that blog.

"Customers buy for their reasons, not yours." - Orvel Ray Wilson

Should a Small Businesses Blog?

I think every small business owner that wants to grow their business should be blogging. If on the other hand you can't commit to regular blog postings then no, you should not have a blog for your business. Blogging takes commitment and the payback can be great!

Blog marketing is a fast growing business marketing strategy that has become a powerful marketing strategy. What should you expect to gain from business blogging?

Postings with interesting and timely information will position you as a knowledgeable expert in your market.

Readers will develop an interest in your products and services. Regular blogging develops familiarity and trust in what you have to say.

Over time this will develop a stream of qualified leads and an increase in sales.

What should small business owners be blogging about? Well, the real answer is just about anything that your customers or prospects would be interested in.

Realtors may want to talk about their local market, trends, days on market, etc. They could write about specific properties to encourage prospective buyers. They could write about the local area for potential relocation clients. The key is to write about subjects of interest for potential customers.

For property managers, they can talk about the rental market, vacancy rates and amenities that are most sought after. They can publish special deals to promote rentals in the off season… you get the idea.

The key thing to do is to create a blog marketing strategy for your business and then follow through. We offer blog marketing assistance and can help you launch a blog for your small business.

"Good communication is as stimulating as black coffee, and just as hard to sleep after." - Anne Morrow Lindbergh

Engaging With Customers

A key challenge for businesses today is how to engage customers. This is important for companies large and small. Conversations are an excellent way for businesses to engage customers. Business blog marketing is more like a conversation while a typical website is more like making an announcement.

Blog marketing is different: Blogging is talking with your audience and allowing them to talk back. It is about listening and learning. This affects what you have to say in your next posting. The idea is to constantly engage your audience to create a mutually beneficial relationship.

Comment Actively: Visit and actively comment on other related blogs. Actively engage bloggers by commenting on key business topics. This will also help you understand your audience's perspective that is related to your product and company.

Engage thru conversation: Conversational marketing is different than traditional marketing. The idea is to create and improve understanding. It is not about merely delivering a message. It is not about making announcements; it is about talking and listening.

Focus on benefits: Customers want to know what you can do for them. How will your product benefit them? Many business managers and owners have difficulty in distinguishing benefits from features. Communications should focus on the benefits you offer.

Point of view: In Internet marketing and in websites, look at the customer experience from an emotional view point. What interests them? What frustrates them? What are the unasked questions? Designing a great customer experience from an emotional angle can have a dramatic improvement on revenue.

"Your customers want you to adapt to them, not the other way round." -Bryan Eisenberg

Blog Networking Through Commenting

One of the best promotional strategies you can have for your blog is making perceptive comments on other blogs. Posting relevant comments on related blogs is like chatting at a networking event. By visiting related blogs and engaging others, you are networking with your peers.

Visit blogs where your targeted visitor is likely to visit. In other words… your competition. This also allows you to keep up with what is going on in your market or area of interest. Getting your name "out there" and participating in conversations is essential if you want to become an authority in your niche.

You want to look for relevant blog postings to comment about. Most blogging systems allow you to leave not only your name but also a link to your website or blog. When you leave a comment, you also leave a link back directly to a relevant blog post you've written. Good positive contributions will result in others clicking through to your blog to learn more about you.

Other blog networking tips
1. Visit and comment on popular blogs that have good traffic.
2. Subscribe to key blogs where you want to participate so you can be notified as soon as a new posting is made.

3. Maintain a strong presence in each discussion.
4. Be the first to comment. The first or second person to comment is more visible than the 10th.
5. Quality over quantity. As you network you are building up your online reputation. Concentrate on making quality comments that add to the conversation.
6. Blogging etiquette: On someone else's blog, you are the guest and not the host. Focus on being more considerate than courageous.

Blogs and Branding

Branding is a huge issue in Internet marketing; it is about making your business unforgettable. Blogs do this by putting your company name, brand name or your name out in front of readers regularly. Familiar brand names create positive emotional responses in the brain such as safety, security, comfort and happiness. After all, people want to do business with people and businesses that they know and trust.

Effective blogging will:
1. Build name recognition
2. Cultivate your brands image
3. Act as an effective PR tool
4. Build trust among readers
5. Improve brand visibility
6. Show your company personality

Successful branding will create an image that will be remembered, and that will allow easy recall.

Blog Writing

Write with purpose and with the consumer in mind. Give people a reason to trust your writing. The easiest way to accomplish that is to provide value. Help them by providing information that they can put to use and use immediately.

Write postings that are interesting. Blog writing that is dull or mundane will not build readership and will limit the effectiveness of your branding effort.

Update your blog regularly and post information that can be interesting and important to your prospective customers. Do not stop at showcasing your products and services, or explaining your company name.

Building your brand has two parts: Recognition and Feeling. Repeated and regular postings will build up the recognition. Building up the emotional side of your branding is equally important. After all, some brands just make us feel good. When your prospects recall your brand, it should make them smile.

Branding Your Business as the Authority

The ultimate prize in any market goes to the business viewed as the authority. Business blogging with interesting and timely information will position you as the knowledgeable expert in your market.

What are readers looking for from their blogging experts? They are looking for someone who stands out from the crowd. They are looking for someone who writes with personality. They are looking for an authoritative voice willing to give opinions, not just repeat what others have said.

They expect new, useful information and clear interpretations of current situations. They want to hear personal preferences, critical opinions and judgments.

What results will you see?

1. **Increase in blog traffic:** When you are considered an expert in your area, you become the leader. Audiences will follow your blog to learn the latest information and to give them ideas for their websites, businesses and blogs.

2. **Become a link magnet:** If what you say is important, others will link to you to support what they are saying. Search engines give great importance to sites that receive lots of links. This improves your rankings, long-term traffic and your perceived importance.

3. **Word-of-mouth recommendations:** People recommend businesses they know and respect. Authority blogs dominate when it comes to those that are new to a topic and need information and support. You will get qualified prospects to call and talk about your services.

4. **Ability to sell ad space:** Authority blogs are sought after for website advertising not only based on traffic levels, but because they are the perceived leader.

"A brand for a company is like a reputation for a person. You earn reputation by trying to do hard things well." - Jeff Bezos

Corporate Blogs

Corporate blogs are business blogs for larger organizations. They help put a human face on the company allowing for direct communication and discussion. The corporate blog helps companies reach their organizational goals.

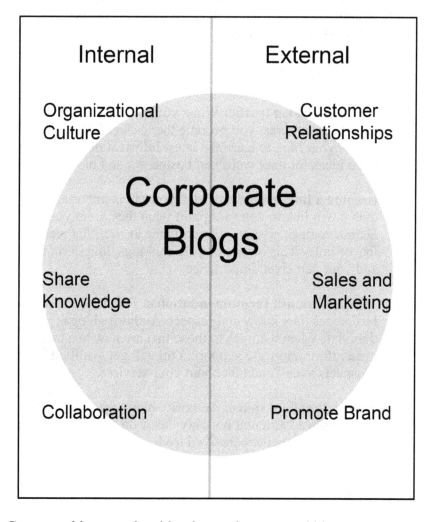

Corporate blogs can be either internal or external blogs.

Internal blogs are used as a communication tool within the organization. They are usually placed on the company Intranet where only employees can view. These can be used in lieu of meetings and e-mail discussions. They are very effective when schedules or employee locations make meetings impractical. Ideas can be categorized by topic, person and date, making archiving ideas and conversations easy.

Frequent uses: Build and strengthen organizational culture, communicate company knowledge and provide teams with an effective collaboration tool.

External blogs are a new public relations tool being used to engage the customer community. These are publicly viewable sites that act as a window into the company itself. They make product announcements, explain policies, rally support, react to criticism and communicate to the outside world. There is also a special type of external blog, the CEO Blog where the CEO communicates directly to the outside world.

Frequent uses: To strengthen the brand, to build and strengthen relationships and to market or sell products and services.

Companies that develop a good corporate blogging strategy are able to capture the goodwill of their community. Companies that connect with their audience and provide real value develop a loyal following. Companies that engage with their customers are able to harness the power of new ideas and feedback. Rewards include sales gains and a positive brand image. Corporate blogs really are the new PR.

Corporate Blogs: The Blogging Policy

Blogging is a powerful communications tool that is being used by businesses large and small. Blogging can pose a serious risk to information security without guidelines. It is essential to have a blogging policy that makes employees aware of what kinds of things can and cannot be discussed in either company blogs or their own private blogs.

Not having a corporate blogging policy allows your employees to cross the line even if they do not have those intentions. Taboo subjects usually include proprietary and confidential information.

What should be said to employees in a basic blogging policy?
1) You are personally responsible for what you write.
2) Follow existing company policies and rules.
3) Keep our confidential information a secret.
4) Use restraint, respect and etiquette.
5) Show respect for the company, its customers, its vendors and employees.
6) In blogging you must add value, be accurate and write about what you know.
7) You must follow all related laws to blogging; (SEC rules on public disclosure, copyright, etc.)

Examples from Corporate Blogging Policies
1) **Place boundaries** on what can be discussed. As an example, Direct2Dell does not allow postings dealing with political, legal or financial matters. They do not allow discussions unrelated to their business.
2) **Don't disclose secrets**. Sun Microsystems advises their employees to use common sense in what they blog about. Employees are responsible for protecting proprietary and confidential information.
3) **Use a disclaimer**. IBM requires employees to disclose that views and opinions presented in the blog are not necessarily those of IBM. This is for all blogs; personal or corporate.
4) **Prior Approval**. The US Army now allows soldiers to blog without prior approval if their topic is not related to the military and they are not using military equipment.

Real Estate Blog Marketing

One of the largest areas of business blog marketing is in real estate. This includes Realtors, mortgage loan brokers, home inspectors and appraisers. Blog marketing is a powerful tool because about 80% of potential real estate clients use the Internet to conduct research.

How to reach your targeted audience? You need to regularly write content that is interesting to your targeted customer. If you market to a very specific area, community or town, then this is what you need to write about.

People read to find local information. Real estate blogs that are written around self promotion tend to turn off readers and have a high bounce rate. Real estate blogs that are great resources write about local events, activities, history, statistics, schools, shopping and jobs. They develop a following of loyal readers.

Successful real estate blogs start with a plan. They identify the primary objective of what the blog needs to accomplish. This can include things such as branding, search engine optimization or lead generation.

Next identify your targeted audience in terms of location and demographics. What do you know about them? What are they interested in? What kinds of things do they want to read about?

Develop your content plan. If your focus is on the relocation market segment, they are most interested in local area information. Local sellers will want to know about valuation and how to prepare their property for sale.

By presenting useful and interesting materials, you become a useful resource to your prospective client. Write really good stuff and they will bookmark your blog or subscribe to your feed and be waiting to hear what you have to say.

"Strategy without tactics is the slowest route to victory. Tactics without strategy is the noise before defeat." Sun Tzu Circa 500 BC

Spam, Splogs and Comment Spam

Spam in all its forms is a costly problem to business. Spam is considered to be unsolicited junk messages that are usually designed to sell or promote something. Spamming can mean using unethical tactics to get high search engine rankings. Spam continues to plague the Internet in the forms of email spam, spam blogs (splogs) and comment spam.

Email spam is a time waster to businesses. Most use extensive filtering software to eliminate email before it arrives. As an example, at our web servers, out of 25,000 incoming emails, 20,000 were tagged as "definitely spam" and deleted before being delivered. Secondary filters identified and filtered an additional 3500 spam email. This means 94% of all incoming email on our server is actual spam and only 6% was legitimate emails.

Spam problems have made traditional email newsletters much less effective. They either don't make it thru to recipients or people are overwhelmed with spam and don't read them. Business Blog Marketing is now a much more effective way of reaching and communicating with your audience. They can either find you thru searching or subscribe for delivery by email or their feed reader.

Spam blogs or splogs, automatically extract information from RSS feeds and re-publish the posting. These are low-cost automated sites that usually make their money by getting viewers to click on ads on the splog site. These damage the original blog poster by stealing content and they are a problem to blog readers because they contain random links and content that turn out to be junk and a waste of time to visit.

Comment spam is a major problem like email spam where automated bots place promotional comments on random blogs in an effort to promote a product, service or website. Much like email spam, spam filters remove a high percentage of this nuisance.

Spam is the scourge of the Internet. Filters, blacklists and penalties from the search engines help keep this in check, but these are still major issues we must deal with.

"Like almost everyone who uses e-mail, I receive a ton of spam every day. Much of it offers to help me get out of debt or get rich quick. It would be funny if it weren't so exciting." - Bill Gates

Business Blogging is replacing HTML eNewsletters!

In this Web 2.0 world many marketers are switching to business blogging either instead of, or in addition to eNewsletters. If you are debating whether to launch a great looking HTML eNewsletter or to start a blog; choose the blog.

Blogs are in contrast less intrusive than email newsletters. They are much faster to produce than an HTML newsletter. History and archiving are automatic. Blogs can be made either private or public. Blogs allow comments and feedback while newsletters do not. eNewsletters are only sent to those on your list, Blogs are published by RSS feed and attract new prospects that you may not have reached.

People are becoming overwhelmed with email spam. HTML newsletters get caught in spam traps. Newsletters take more planning and longer to produce. You must check your links, send test copies and otherwise correctly configure your HTML newsletter.

Remember, the marketing strategy of a business blog is similar to that of an eNewsletter. They both build credibility and an ongoing relationship with your customers and prospects. They keep your product or service first in their mind when they're ready to buy.

Because blogs allow you to post fresh content almost instantly, they are more up to date and allow you to greatly accelerate your marketing effort.

How much is My Website Worth?

A website or blog is worth exactly what someone is willing to pay for it. This is just like valuing any business that you may want to sell. There are many formulas and factors that go into a valuation. It also depends if it is an eCommerce website, an informational website or a blog.

In buying or selling any business, one of the biggest determiners of value is gross revenue rather than net profit. This is because the buyer of a business can make changes to improve profitability, but it is much harder to change sales volume. A typical business is valued between 50% and 200% of total annual sales. The final value is based on industry, asset values, profitability and future cash flows.

Website Valuation Methods

Revenue method: For websites that have an income stream such as eCommerce, Google Adsense or other advertising, the business valuation model using 50% and 200% of total annual sales is pretty accurate. I always start using one year (100%).

Factors that affect valuation include website architecture, SEO, visitor traffic, traffic sources, Google PageRank, branding, industry stature, content quality, diversity of income streams and income potential.

Traffic Method: Use the average PPC values for (top 10 placements) the primary keyword phrases and multiply this times the average yearly traffic to get an estimated value.

A website that receives 15,000 visitors per year with an average PPC value of 35 cents per click would have an estimated value of $5250.

Creation Method: What would it cost to recreate the website including design, SEO and programming costs? This is generally the most conservative of the valuation methods.

Usually a combination of all 3 methods is used. You may use 50% of the revenue method, plus 30% of the traffic method plus 20% of the creation method. This gives a starting point. The final price is always determined through negotiation between buyer and seller.

"It is not so important to know everything as to know the exact VALUE of everything, to appreciate what we learn, and to arrange what we know."- Hannah More

Earn Money While Blogging

There are a number of ways to add income streams to your blog. You can even turn blogging into a successful home based business.

Adding Income Streams
This requires that you develop a regular readership and site traffic to generate income. These can range from developing a little extra spending money to some serious revenue.

1. **Google Adsense**: These are context relevant search engine ads where you are paid every time someone clicks on one of the ads.
2. **Blog Ads**: If your site has a large amount of traffic, BlogAds lets you join its database. You are paid for the ad

space on a monthly basis.

3. **Text Link Ads**: Once your blog has a decent PageRank, sell one-way text links to webmasters who have niche relevant websites.

4. **Sell Products**: Services such as Café Press allow you to sell all sorts of merchandise with your logo on it. This includes t-shirts, cups, caps, etc.

5. **Affiliate Programs**: Be a middle man! Receive a commission every time one of your readers ends up buying. This includes companies like Amazon.

6. **Donation Button**: Add a donation button connected to your PayPal account. Ask your readers for support if your blog supports a cause.

Get Paid for Writing

1. **Pay Per Post:** Contract to write postings on your own blog. This can include product reviews and postings with links to sponsored websites. You can get writing assignments from services such as PayPerPost, Review Me and LoudLaunch.

2. **Niche Blogs**: Create a series of niche blogs and you can increase your contract writing to a full time job. Each blog should be targeted for a particular topic that you are comfortable writing about.

3. **Blog Ghost Writer**: Take writing assignments for businesses that don't have the time or skills to write their own basic blog content.

5 Business Blogging Myths Debunked

Myth #1 "Blogs are just a fad and will soon pass."

Not true. Blogs have become part of everyday life and will not be going away. There are over 70 million blogs in use today and this number is steadily growing. In the past few years blogging has moved from a personal tool to a marketing tool.

Myth #2 "My customers don't read blogs."
Not true. It is estimated that in the US 27% of the people read blogs on a regular basis. In a recent survey, information from blogs is more useful than information from newspapers, radio or television. If your customers use the Internet, many of the search results they read are from blogs.

Myth #3 "People will make negative comments and hurt my business."
Not true. With the web, there are many ways for customers to vent their anger and frustration about your products and services. It is much better to be able to address and respond to a problem. How you address problems can help win new converts. You have the option of allowing or rejecting comments that are unreasonable.

Myth #4 "If I have a normal website I don't need a blog."
Not true. Blogs allow you to reach new audiences. Each posting is sent out to the web using RSS much the way news stories are sent. Internet marketing today is much stronger when businesses use both a website and a blog.

Myth #5 "Business blogs are the magic solution."
Not true. Blogs are another marketing tool that can be very effective... they are not magic. To be successful they take planning and writing articles that your targeted market find interesting. Blogs are a very powerful marketing tool when used correctly.

"The secret to managing is to keep the guys who hate you away from the guys who are undecided." - Casey Stengel

Chapter 3 Trends in Blogging
Social Media Now Important to Business Marketing

Blog marketing has gone main stream according to a study by The University of Massachusetts-Dartmouth's Center for Marketing Research. The Inc 500 companies are marketing with blogs, social networking and podcasts at a rate more than double that of Fortune 500 companies. Inc 500 companies are those on Inc magazine's annual list of the 500 fastest growing privately-owned companies.

What media is important?
121 companies were surveyed and 66% reported social media as playing an important or very important role in business and marketing strategies. Social networking and Blog marketing are being accepted and implemented at a rate far faster than expected.

Companies were also asked about their actual usage of the various types of social media.

Message boards 33%
Social networking.. 27%
Online video 24%
Blogs... 19%
Wikis 17%
Podcasting 11%

What areas are being budgeted for in the marketing budgets? The single largest strategy is blog marketing at (42%) of the responding companies. This was followed by social networking (40%) and adding RSS feeds at (37%).

The main reason more businesses are blogging is because the tool costs little or nothing to use, which is attractive to businesses with small marketing budgets. Additionally, it is a good way to

Biz Blog Marketing

be heard and stand out from the crowd.

"Blogs are tailor-made for small businesses, and they are a better tool for them," said Anita Campbell, editor of the blog Small Business Trends.

Blog Marketing: Fast Growing Trend for Businesses

Blog marketing using business blogs is the hot new frontier in Internet marketing. Blogging gives businesses a new access to potential and existing customers. But how much is this growing?

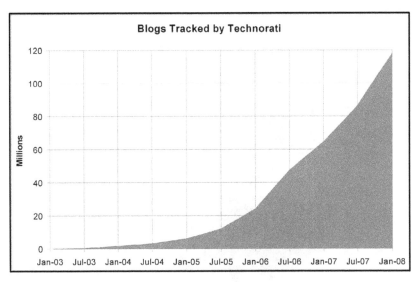

Source of Data: Technorati.com

Technorati is known widely for its quarterly State of the Blogosphere reports, analyzing the trends around blogs and blogging. These are some excerpts from Technorati's <u>April 2007</u> report.

Technorati was then tracking over 70 million weblogs, (by the end of 2007 this had risen to about 115 million) and we're seeing about 175,000 new weblogs being created worldwide each day. That's about 1.4 blogs created every second of every day.

One interesting item to note in April 2007, the number of blogs in the top 100 most popular websites has risen substantially. During Q3 2006 there were only 12 blogs in the Top 100 most popular sites. In Q4, however, there were 22 blogs on the list — further evidence of the continuing maturation of the Blogosphere.

In terms of blog posts by language, Japanese retakes the top spot from our last report, with 37% (up from 33%) of the posts followed closely by English at 36% (down from 39%).

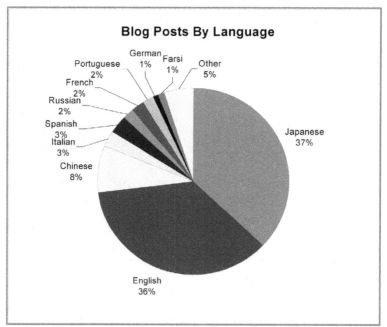

Blog Posts By Language

German 1% · Farsi 1% · Portuguese 2% · French 2% · Russian 2% · Spanish 3% · Italian 3% · Chinese 8% · Other 5% · Japanese 37% · English 36%

Source: Technorati.com based on Q4 2006.

Businesses are quickly taking on Blog marketing as a mainstream Internet marketing strategy and are reaping the rewards in terms of new inquiries, customers and business.

*"We should all be concerned about the future because we will
have to live the rest of our lives there."* - Charles F. Kettering

Web 2.0 Internet, the Next Generation

Web 2.0 an umbrella term first coined in 2003 by O'Reilly Media
that meant the second generation of the web. This second
generation is defined by a new more powerful interactive web.
The first is the interactive use of social networking, blogs and
wikis. The second is new technologies such as Ajax which allows
web applications to work more like desktop software. Web 2.0
presents new challenges and opportunities for Internet marketing
strategies.

Web 2.0 includes the change from individual isolated websites to
blogging with RSS feeds to quickly broadcast and allow
responses. Content management systems were prominent in web
1.0 and then Wikis came into being allowing web users to update
content. Web 2.0 has been made more powerful with Ajax which
allows web applications such as Google maps to function.

The Participatory Web

Web 2.0 is marked by a social interaction. Weblogs, or "blogs,"
as they are called are easily created and updated by those with
even a minimum of technology know-how. Blogs make use of
RSS (Real Simple Syndication). This allows blogs to use XML
feeds to broadcast postings across the Internet in a very short
time. Blogging has moved from 3 million in 2004 to 115 million
blogs (end of 2007) being tracked by Technorati.

A Wiki is a website that allows visitors to add, remove, and edit
content. The word wiki is a Hawaiian word meaning "quick."
Wikis are generally designed with the philosophy of making it

easy to correct mistakes, rather than making it difficult to make them. The English-language Wikipedia has the largest user base among all wikis.

Ajax

Ajax is a newer technology that allows web applications to work in real time without the continual need for refreshing content. Ajax is short for Asynchronous Java-Script + XML. This works by introducing an intermediary Ajax engine between the user and the server. Instead of loading a web-page, at the start of the session, the browser loads an Ajax engine written in Java-Script and is usually tucked away in a hidden frame. So the user is never staring at a blank browser window and an hourglass icon, waiting around for the server to do something.

Web 2.0 may have started out as more marketing hype, but it has evolved into a real way to describe the evolution of the web. The web continues to evolve and change. Businesses need to evaluate their web design and SEO strategies to make use of Web 2.0. So when will Web 3.0 be here?

Human Needs Drive Web 2.0

What defines Web 2.0, is it the technology or the human side? We tend to talk about the technology such as RSS, blogs, wikis, AJAX, XML and APIs. Although technology is important, this transformation is really sparked by human needs.

Web 2.0 is about collaboration, sharing, connecting, expressing and interacting. With web 2.0, the Internet is being woven into the social fabric of today's society. Web 1.0 was more about technology and Web 2.0 is about the integration of this technology into the basic needs of our daily lives.

Collaboration: Rather than working alone, tools like wikis allow people to work together. Wikis and other Web 2.0 tools allow companies to develop and communicate policies and procedures and to collaborate with customers and partners.

Sharing: No need to read an online magazine or news feed alone, the web allows interaction and sharing with others. Sites today allow easy sharing of opinions (blogs), photos, videos and even your favorite web links.

Connecting: The technology tools of Web 2.0 allow people to connect and interact in their common interests. Social networks connect and collaborate in real time. It is about connecting people and developing a network approach to business.

Expressing: Blogging is a way of human expression. People can express their opinions on just about anything. The Web 2.0 spaces such as MySpace and YouTube allow for easy expression, participation and representation.

Interacting: People want human interaction. Web 2.0 has brought in conversational marketing. Companies now hold a two way dialog with their customers thru blogs, real time chat and instant messenger.

"Ask yourself the secret of your success. Listen to your answer, and practice it." - Richard Bach

What Will Web 3.0 Mean?

Even as Web 2.0 is becoming accepted, the debates are raging over what Web 3.0 will be. More importantly, how Web 3.0 will impact both consumers and businesses on the web. If Web 2.0 is taken as the "read-write" web, then Web 3.0 will be the "data" web.

It is important to remember that changes in the web are evolutionary not revolutionary. Past trends will continue and new technologies will become available at an even faster rate.

So what is the vision for Web 3.0? Information access will be easier as the "Semantic Web" is being developed. Web software agents will find, share and integrate information for searches and according to user profiles. Data will be made available from multiple sources simultaneously and applications will speak to each other directly, and for broader searches for information.

This means you may be able to search for all the hard to find ingredients for a recipe and locate the closest store that carries all of them. You will be able look at available fashions from multiple stores just in your size.

Other visions for Web 3.0 include 10 megabits of bandwidth all the time. This would make video available all the time. This would create the "video web."

Social networking in the form of blogging is expected to have continued growth and be very important to both consumers and businesses. Web 3.0 is certain to bring more information together faster for consumers. Businesses will need to be evolving and changing if they expect to be leaders in their market.

Blogging + Video = Vlogging

The simplest form of video blogging, or vlogging, means putting a video file online, linking to it from your blog. These are blogs that primarily feature video shorts instead of text. Just like blogs, vlogging started as a video version of a diary.

Vlogging has evolved into a short video format that could include anything from comedy sketches, to fictional drama to video opinions. Any subject that can be blogged about can be put into a video version and become a vlog.

The fact is that there are a large number of blogs now, but only a tiny percentage of those use video as a means to further market their businesses or themselves. Just as it has become common for a business to have a blog, using video to promote their brand or educate will become common.

History: Video blogging started its move forward in 2004 when Jay Dedman started the Yahoo! Videoblogging Group. Vlogging saw a strong increase in popularity beginning in the year 2005 when the videoblogger conference was held in New York City. YouTube, a popular video sharing website was created in early 2005.

Still in its infancy, the number of vlogs was recorded at just 23,000 in early 2007.

Video Podcasting: For video podcasting, you must publish your vlog in either the FLV (Flash Video) or SWF (Shockwave Flash) file formats. You can get your "vlog" accepted by Apple's iTunes so their subscribers can find and subscribe to your vlog (which gives you access to 19 million users at last count).

Micro-Blogging

Micro-Blogging is one of the newest forms of blogging. Micro-blogging allows people to blog from mobile devices using text messaging. It's regularly publishing small pieces of content on the web. This form of blogging is usually limited to 140 characters per entry. This can be done using instant messaging software or a cell phone.

Micro-blogging allows posting of short thoughts and ideas to a personal blog or a Micro business blog. This is actually closer to a good blog comment then a well formed full blog posting. It is a more immediate and spontaneous form of blogging.

The three popular Micro-Blogging services today are Twitter, Jaiku and Pownce.

1. **Twitter:** Founded as a San Francisco start-up in March 2006 and launched as a product in July 2006. Twitter is the most popular of this form of social networking.
2. **Jaiku:** This is the primary competitor to Twitter. Jaiku goes a step further by serving as a mobile RSS aggregator.
3. **Pownce:** Which is Digg's founder Kevin Rose's latest venture. Pownce is the latest entry and has learned from Twitter and Jaiku with even greater functionality. It even lets you attach mp3 and download links to a message.

What can you say in 140 characters? "Web 2.0 is turning to Micro-blogging. It forces bloggers to be brief and to the point. Ideas are now being provided in smaller micro-chunks." –*This is 140 Characters*

On micro business blogging: "So what if your company's blog only reaches a few dozen people a day. If they're the right people, the payoff is obvious." -*124 characters* – By Seth Godin

Blog Reader Demographics

A key part of business blog marketing is to understand your readership and potential prospects. There are about 1.5 million new blog postings each day.

Blog readers tend to be early adopters and influencers. They are more likely to take an action such as calling or emailing as a result of what they have read. It is estimated that in the US 27% of the people read blogs on a regular basis.

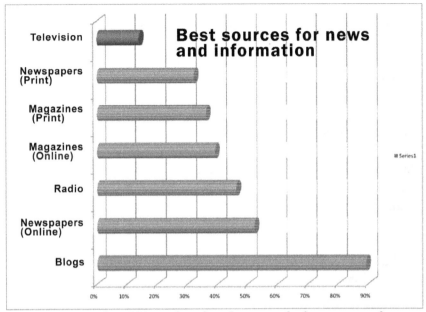

BlogAds surveyed 35,000 readers for what were the best sources for useful information. Blogs were clearly the number one trusted source.

Blogads.com has an ongoing blog readership project and in 2006 they surveyed over 35,000 or their readers.

- o 62% of their readers are over 40
- o 72% were male
- o 66% had a family income over $60,000
- o 39% had households of 3 or more
- o 78% were college graduates
- o Top categories for online purchases were plane tickets, computers and consumer electronics.
- o 82% do not have their own blog
- o 67% read 5 or more blogs each day

Among blog readers, the most common occupations:

Retired 8.8%
Computer professional 8.7%
Educator 6.3%
Student 5.7%
Lawyer/Judge 5.0%

The most common industries were:
Education 14%
Computers 11%
Legal 7%
Health Care 6%
Government 5%

Media with useful (or extremely useful) sources of news and information:
Blogs 89%
Newspapers (online) 52%
Radio 46%
Magazines (online) 39%
Magazines (print) 36%
Newspapers (print) 32%
Television 14%

Ghost Blog Writing

In business and corporate communications ghost writers or copywriters have long been used. Businesses use copywriters to prepare speeches, write letters from the president, annual reports, create press releases and write website content. Should ghost blog writers be used for business blog marketing?

This is an area that is currently being hotly debated around the Internet. Blogs are viewed as the platform where the authentic human voice must be heard. Blogs are more trusted than other forms of media such as newspapers, radio and TV. They are where people turn for real opinions that are not filtered thru the corporate PR department.

On the other hand, blogs are part of mainstream business marketing as a way of reaching new customers and better communicating with current customers. There is no denying the power of business blogging as a search marketing tool.

With business blogging becoming a part of most marketing departments, the use of copywriters in blogging is here to stay. Whether it is a CEO that has a staff member write material for tomorrow's posting or an outside agency writing marketing articles.

Businesses simply need a blog to be competitive in today's world. Many business owners and senior managers have important things to say and lack the skills to communicate well in a blog format.

A speech writer must research topics, understand positions and opinions to help their clients be clearly understood in the same way a blog ghost writer must carefully research and understand their client to layout case studies and other important marketing messages.

For businesses, the focus is on their products, their services and what it is that they are selling. It's not about the individual. Blog ghost writing helps businesses communicate their ideas.

Podcasting

Podcasting is online audio or video content that is delivered via an RSS feed. This technology gives listeners and viewers content on-demand. It works much the same way as syndication of other blog content.

The consumer finds topics that interest them and subscribes. They use a type of software known as an aggregator, sometimes called a podcatcher to manage these feeds. This works very much like a blog feed reader.

These can be downloaded to a mobile player or viewed directly on the computer. In 2006 it was estimated that 80% of podcasts were viewed or listened to directly on the PC where they were downloaded and never transferred to a mobile player.

In a 2007 survey, approximately 13% of all people have listened to one or more podcasts and this number is growing. The survey found more listeners 55+ than in the 18-24 age group. Podcast users are twice as likely to have incomes over 100K and nearly twice as likely to have incomes between 75K and 100K.

Owners of small businesses are finding that podcasts are an effective way to access or present information in a cost effective manner. 2007 forecasted sales for MP3 players are 120 million and 200 million for MP3 enabled cell phones. The potential market for podcasts continues to grow at a strong pace.

Podcast marketing is a form of broadcast marketing and this type of strategy reaches a wider audience. Podcasts can be both Audio & Video and reach viewers who are looking for an alternative to reading web pages for information.

Blog Networks

A Blog network is a group of blogs that are linked together under a common brand name, domain name or traffic referral system. Although there are different models, their chief purpose can be to promote blogs or to serve as an outlet for business advertising.

Commercial blog networks and Independent blog networks act as an outlet for blog advertisers. These are corporations and businesses that want to promote websites, products and services in the blogosphere. This form of advertising is highly targeted by choosing blogs aligned with their market niche.

For advertisers: Networks serve as a way to reach a whole new audience. They allow a way for businesses that may not have their own business blog to still promote their company. They allow businesses a chance to get valuable content links from blogs to their websites.

For bloggers: Networks serve as a way to earn money using their writing skills. This is a way for freelance writers to launch their own business. This is a way people are making full time livings by blogging each and every day. Networks are searching for passionate writers who can produce quality niche content.

Types of Networks

Commercial Blog Networks: Here the organization owns the blogs and hires writers to create blog postings. They normally sell advertising. Examples are engadget.com and b5media.com.

Independent Blog Networks: Here the bloggers own the blogs and the network acts as a marketplace putting bloggers and advertisers together. Examples are payperpost.com and loudlaunch.com.

Affiliate Blog Networks: This is a group of blogs that share a common interest. Bloggers own their own blogs and they are bound together by a common interest, hobby or politics. They are really a federation of like-minded bloggers.

Delicious.com (Del.icio.us)

The social bookmarking website del.icio.us (pronounced as "delicious") is an extremely popular web 2.0 website. In

September 2007, it was announced that the website name would be changing to Delicious.com. Today, both domain names will get you to the same site.

This is a free service. The site was founded by Joshua Schachter in September 2003, and was acquired by Yahoo! in 2005.

Del.icio.us allows individuals to quickly bookmark new and relevant websites to a central online database. These are sites that they find valuable. At the same time, users enter tags or keywords that describe the bookmarked site. This allows people to search their bookmarks by keywords. These bookmarks can be accessed from any computer. This is great for people who use multiple computers between work, school and home.

What makes Delicious.com a social bookmarking website is that anyone can go in and see which sites are being bookmarked by others. These bookmarks are searchable because each person has entered a brief tag that describes the bookmarked website.

What I like best is that it is a very effective research tool for business blog marketing articles. By using the search features on del.icio.us, you can quickly get a list of relevant high quality sites that others thought important enough to bookmark.

The benefit for researchers is to see which sites are most popular. This eliminates the low quality results that you get with typical searches. The tag system used makes it easy to find highly relevant results for whatever topic you are researching.

Due to its popularity, some people have started using Del.icio.us as a traffic building tool along with search engine optimization. A website becomes more visible the more often it is submitted and tagged.

Digg.com

Digg is a community-based popularity website that ranks articles based on popular opinion. Anyone can join and influence these results. News stories and websites are submitted by members, and then can be promoted to the front page through a user-based voting or ranking system. People can ignore or bury bad stories and promote good ones.

First launched in December of 2004 as an experiment, Digg was created by Kevin Rose, Owen Byrne and Jay Adelson. Digg started with the idea to use online polling as a way to know which news stories are the most important to readers and the idea has grown from there.

How it works
Any registered Digg member finds an article, video, or podcast online and submits it to Digg.com. As of March 2007, there were 1 million registered Digg members. This story immediately appears in "Upcoming Stories" where other members find it and if they "Digg it," the story moves up in popularity.

Top stories move to the website front page. When it moves to the front page, there is an enormous surge in traffic as people go and see what the buzz is all about.

On the front page of Digg.com there is a list of postings and news stories where members can easily follow links to the postings, make comments and if they like it they can Digg it, or if they don't, they can bury it.

Home page screenshot taken from Digg.com

Adding a "Digg" button to your blog makes it easy for registered Digg members to submit your blog posting and possibly turn the story you wrote into the next major breaking story. This can quickly reward great postings with a large amount of visitor traffic.

Technorati

Technorati is an Internet Search Engine that is dedicated to blogs. They closely watch the blogosphere and report all types of blogging trends and statistics. They post a tag cloud on their home page that shows the hot topics of the day.

Founded in 2002 by David Sifry, Technorati was originally a set of web services focused on the newly forming blogosphere. They have grown and developed into one of the major forces in blogging. Their name is a combination of technology and literati (Intellectuals). As of the end of 2007 they were tracking about 115 million blogs.

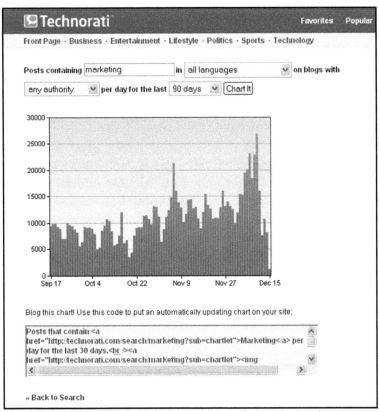

Technorati.com not only has graphs of how often a given phrase is used, but they allow these graphs to be embedded in websites and blogs.

Technorati is an important place to have your blog registered. Once your blog is "claimed," Technorati gets information from your blog whenever you post. They are continually indexing the live web. Blog postings are incorporated into search within minutes of being posted. Technorati is one of the best traffic sources for blogs.

Technorati introduced tags as a method for categorizing posts. A tag is really a simple category name that describes a posting. By using tags, you can bring people to your blog who are searching for certain things.

Technorati Authority: is the number of blogs (not links) linking to a website in the last six months. The higher the number, the more Authority the blog has.

Technorati Ranking: Technorati Rank is calculated based on how far your blog is from the top. The blog with the highest Technorati Authority is the #1 ranked blog. Technorati has a list of the top 100 most popular blogs (http://technorati.com/pop/blogs/)

"Information is recorded in vast interconnecting NETWORKs. Each idea or image has hundreds, perhaps thousands, of associations and is connected to numerous other points in the mental NETWORK." - Peter Russell

Chapter 4 Marketing and Internet Marketing

Internet marketing is the use of the Internet to promote, advertise and sell products and services. Blog marketing is a part of Internet marketing just as Internet marketing is part of the overall marketing plan. A strategic Internet marketing plan is similar to a strategic business marketing plan, just with a narrower focus.

In building your blog marketing plan, you need to think about how this fits into your business objectives and other marketing strategies. They should all interrelate and work together.

We do this planning with our clients in a drill down approach. Even if no formal plan exists, we will talk thru the key elements in a short time... usually in under an hour.

Business Plan: Describe your company and its history. What are your short and long-term business objectives? What services or products do you sell?

Marketing Plan: What market do you compete in? Describe your primary competitors along with their strengths and weaknesses. Who are your customers and on what basis do they make their buying decision? What are your branding, positioning and pricing strategies?

Internet Marketing: Based on your marketing plan, what are your online objectives in terms of targeted traffic, selling, lead generation, customer service or warranty service? Develop strategies around website marketing, search engine marketing, blog marketing, email marketing, affiliate marketing and podcast marketing.

Blog Marketing: Based on your targeted customer, what interesting content can you present to develop readership? Use your blog to support your other Internet strategies and marketing plans.

**Relationship of Internet Marketing
to the Business Plan**

Internet marketing is part of the marketing plan, which is a key part of the business plan. All parts should be coordinated and focused to get the best results.

"The beginning is the most important part of the work." - Plato

Writing a Marketing Plan

A Marketing plan is really a mini business plan that emphasizes the market analysis and marketing strategies along with the budgets and financials to show the expected results. So, what goes into a typical formal marketing plan?

Executive Summary (2-3 pages)
Keep it short, 3 pages tops. You have to make the opportunity clear and establish your company's key advantage over the competition. State the purpose of the plan succinctly. The summary must be persuasive in conveying the company's growth and profit potential.

Company Overview (1-2 pages)
Tell your story. What is it that makes your firm unique? Describe the product or service you specialize in and the markets you serve. Talk about what your enterprise does, the legal form of your company, and what stage of development you are in.

Product or Service (1-2 pages)
List products/services and briefly describe each in order of highest sales or significance. Describe in understandable terms. Where is each product/service in its life cycle (introductory, growth, maturity)? Explain the unique advantages your company enjoys in the marketplace.

Market Analysis (5-7 pages)
The market analysis and then the strategies developed in the next section are the heart of the marketing plan.
1. Define the market, size and growth. What share do you have now? How about in the future?
2. Profile your competitors discussing their market share, strengths and weaknesses.
3. How is your product positioned in the market and how does it stack up against the competition?
4. Profile your targeted customers. What drives their buying behavior and what would cause them to select your product / service over your competitor.

66

Marketing Strategies and Tactics (4-6 pages)
Present your company's strategies and tactics to penetrate and capture the market.
1. Basic 3-year strategic plan for the market, products and services, and customer segments.
2. Describe branding and positioning strategies.
3. Explain your marketing and sales strategies you will employ to reach your targeted customer base in terms of pricing, distribution channel and promotion.
4. Discuss advertising, Internet, public relations communications, trade shows, telemarketing, direct mail or any other market and sales plans you intend to employ in promoting and selling your product.
5. Present your sales forecasts.

Financial Budgets and Analysis (3-5 pages)
Include sales history and sales projections by month. Present sales and marketing budgets and budgets for key programs. Show the projected results in terms of net income, cash flow and break even projections. There should be a 1-2 page narrative with assumptions, describing key items in the financials. Support your projections with assumptions.

Products and Services

The Products and services section is what defines your business. The marketing plan focuses on the uniqueness of your product or service. This is the foundation for any business plan, marketing plan or marketing strategy.

Tip: If you are forming a new business select products or services that can be used by one targeted customer. If you are selling products targeted at the do-it-yourself home repair market, then it would make sense to add additional products that fit that same market. This allows you to target your advertising and marketing with a minimum of cost.

What should you talk about in this section? Discuss the features, what makes your offering different and the benefits to the customer. Discuss what the market currently uses and what they need above the current use. What makes this product or service different from all the others? What is it that sets your product or service apart from all the rest?

In light of the competition, why would someone buy from your company? What are future developments that are coming?

Discuss where your product is in the product life cycle (Development, introduction, growth, maturity, and decline). Is this life cycle based on the individual products or is there a fundamental market shift (such as automobiles creating demise of buggy whips)?

Remember that benefits can be intangible as well as tangible; for instance, if you're selling luxury automobiles, your customers will benefit from an enjoyable ride with all the fine comforts. They will also benefit with increased status in the eyes of their friends and clients.

B2B vs. B2C Marketing

How you develop and implement your marketing is fundamentally different for business-to-business (B2B) and business-to-consumer (B2C) customers. They are fundamentally different in how they reach their buying decision.

B2C: marketing
1. Driven by fashion and trends
2. Personal and impulsive buying
3. Single step buying process
4. Shorter sales cycle
5. Emotional buying decision based on status, desire, or price

How Decisions Are Made

B2B   Vs.   B2C

B2B	B2C
Rational	Emotional
Benefits	Popularity
Group Decision	Personal
Multi Step	Single Step

A B2C customer looks at a product and thinks: Do I want this? The B2B customer looks at something and thinks: How does this make sense for the business?

The B2C buyer makes a more impulsive decision based on their current need. This includes product, value, cost, and status. Buying is based on a want with a very short decision making time. Most consumers will buy regularly from stores and locations that they like. In that respect, B2C marketing needs to build trust and loyalty with their customers.

B2B marketing
1. Driven by technological progress
2. Group decision making
3. Multi-step buying process
4. Longer sales cycle
5. Rational buying decision based on business value

Perhaps the biggest difference with the B2B buyer is the sales cycle. Usually many people are involved with the decision to purchase something. The business buyer is typically much more knowledgeable about the product. Business buyers will often spend much time doing analysis before making a decision.

A company marketing to businesses needs to focus on relationship building and communication using marketing activities that generate leads that can be nurtured during the sales cycle.

"Business has only two functions -- marketing and innovation." - Peter F. Drucker

Target Markets

A business can target a broad audience with their marketing, but then you are only going after people who CAN use your product or service. By narrowing the focus to a smaller group you can target people who are LIKELY to buy.

Successful small businesses understand that only a limited number of people will actually buy their products or services. With a limited amount of marketing dollars it is important to focus on the people with the highest probability of buying.

Target marketing involves 3 steps
1. Market segmentation
2. Choosing the target
3. Product positioning

Target marketing contrasts with mass marketing, which offers a single product to the entire market.

Niche Market
A niche market is a narrowly defined, targeted group that has a common interest or need. A good niche market should be large

enough to produce the volume of business you need and yet small enough for your competition to overlook it. They should have a need that you can fill and be a group that you can easily reach with a marketing message.

How do you identify and go after a niche market?
1. **Identify**: Start with your current customers and look for patterns in industry segments, geographic areas or other characteristics.
2. **Where**: Where do they hang out? What do they read? What websites do they go to? Are there mailing lists available? What you are trying to figure out is how to reach them with your marketing campaign.
3. **Reach them**: Your marketing message should be low key and show that you are interested and that you understand their need.

Segmentation

Segmenting is a key step in defining your target or niche market. Businesses that target specialty markets can develop focused strategies to promote their products and services much more effectively than marketing to the "average" customer.

Market segmenting divides up the targeted prospects into logical groups that have similar needs and requirements. These groups are likely to respond to a given marketing approach. Markets can be segmented or targeted using a variety or combination of factors.

Demographic Segmentation
1. Age: Consumer needs and desires change with age. Age categories are typically divided into four segments: child, young adult, adult, and older adult. A shampoo manufacturer may offer products ranging from baby shampoo to shampoo for women over 50.
2. Gender: Marketers use gender segmenting in products such as clothing, magazines, cosmetics and toiletries.

3. <u>Income:</u> Many companies will target affluent customers for luxury goods while others will target lower income levels with outlet stores. Examples are Neiman Marcus targeting the luxury market and Wal-Mart targeting the discount market.

Geographical segmentation: Breaking up customers based on location for multi-national businesses that have regional and national marketing programs to meet their geographical units. This process also works for local pizza delivery companies who plan delivery areas based on population density and delivery routes.

Psychographic segmentation
1. <u>Lifestyles Segmentation</u>: Yuppies are a good example; these were young upwardly mobile professionals. They had buying habits associated with expensive cars, personal electronics, and prestigious jobs.
2. <u>Personality Characteristics</u>: Use this to develop a brand personality. Pigaio motorcycles markets to young 18-25 outgoing, independent persons.
3. <u>Social Class Segmentation</u>: This assumes that the higher your profession the more you will earn and the more affluent lifestyle you will lead. This presumes that your profession does have an impact on the way you behave.

Positioning

Product positioning is the art of tailoring a product or service image to appeal to a particular target market. Positioning is a powerful tool that allows you to create an outward representation or identity. It is the relative comparison to other products in a given market.

Developing a positioning strategy really depends on how competitors position themselves. Developing a "me too" strategy positions yourself close to your competition. You can distance yourself with a direct comparison of how you are different.

Positioning is what the customer believes and not what the marketer wants them to believe. Positioning should be answering the question "Why should I buy?" A good position makes you unique and is considered a benefit by your target market.

The primary elements of positioning are:
1. **Price**: This can range from luxury to a commodity.
2. **Quality**: This includes product, services, warranty and return policies.
3. **Service**: This includes sales, customer service and support.
4. **Distribution**. How easy is it for customers to find and buy your product?

Positioning Examples
1. In 1910 sock maker Holeproof Hosiery Company ran the ad: "To The 5,196,267 Unmarried Men of America" Unmarried men were assumed to be either not capable of, or not interested in, darning socks.
2. Apple computers are positioned as better for design and use graphics more easily than with Windows or UNIX.
3. Although Tiffany and Costco both sell diamonds; Tiffany sells their diamonds based on the highest quality money can buy. Costco tells us that diamonds are diamonds and they offer the best value.
4. Margarine is sold as a healthier and lower cost alternative to butter. Butter on the other hand is marketed as wholesome ingredients and providing better taste.

Market Analysis

The market analysis looks at the potential demand for your product or service. It looks at market size, trends and dynamics. Knowing about the market and how it is currently serviced provides you with important information needed in developing your marketing plan.

The complete marketing analysis has 3 parts:
1. Market Analysis
2. Competitor Analysis
3. Customer Analysis

The market analysis looks at market size, growth rate, profitability and trends. Financial trends, profitability and cost structures as well as typical distribution methods are also examined. The last step is to identify the key factors for success.

Market Size: The market size is measured in either units or value (amount spent by customers) of all sales in a market. Good sources include government data and trade associations.

Market Growth Rate: This can be forecasted based on past trends... Or a better way is by analyzing growth drivers such as demographics and factoring in lifecycles, predicted technology shifts and economic business cycles.

Market Profitability and Industry Cost Structure: There are a number of ways to determine market profitability. The first is to look at the profitability of several public companies in that market or similar markets. The second is to look at income and balance sheet data from websites such as http://basic.bizminer.com.

Market Trends: Researching technology and lifecycle trends thru Internet, trade associations and news databases can give a tremendous insight into coming trends. Watching blog postings and forums are also great resources.

Distribution Channels: Distribution channels move products and services from businesses to consumers. Determine the number of levels (channel partners) that are normal for the target market. What is the mark-up required for each level?

"Before you build a better mousetrap, it helps to know if there are any mice out there." – Author Unknown

Competitor analysis

Looking at competitors in your targeted market gives great insight into what they are doing successfully and unsuccessfully. In forming your own marketing strategies, you have the opportunity to learn from their mistakes and what they are doing right.

Examine the main competitors that serve your same target market. Locate who they are by searching the Internet or looking them up in the yellow pages. Other methods include finding them in the trade journals, asking suppliers that you will be using or by contacting trade associations.

If they are local, visit them as a customer or potential customer. If they are an e-business, visit their web store and comb through it. Search on the web for what others are saying about them. What is their reputation? Talk with suppliers. Locate and talk with your competitor's customers.

You will want to profile 5-10 competitors to learn what they are doing. Prepare a checklist and keep good notes. Your actual checklist will vary according to your industry or market. It is easier to locate information on public than privately held companies.

Competitor Analysis Checklist
1. Background: Location, facilities, ownership, number of employees and history
2. Products and services: Features, attributes, brands
3. Target markets served, market perception, market leadership, growth rates, customer loyalty and market share
4. Pricing strategies
5. Promotion and advertising
6. Online presence: Websites, blogging, search positioning
7. Distribution methods
8. Financial standing: profitability, P-E ratios, financial ratios, liquidity, and cash flow
9. R&D capabilities: patents, licenses
10. Distribution methods

Who is your customer?

Who is the target customer for your product or service? You want to understand everything about them. Understand the needs and desires of your customer. Where do they live? What are their gender, age, income, education and interests? Ultimately, what causes them to make their buying decision?

Successful businesses understand accurate and specific information about their customers and use this to build their marketing strategies. There may be more than one person involved in the decision to buy.

If you sell men's slacks, who do you market to? One study found in retail stores 72% of men buy their own clothes, but in online purchases only 43% of men do their own buying.

If you sell electronic components to an industrial company, who should you be marketing to? The buyer may be the one ordering from you, but it may be the engineer who actually makes the buying decision. Usually, a buyer is interested most in price and delivery, while an engineer will look at performance specifications and reliability. Each would require a different marketing message and would read very different trade journals.

What do you need to know?
1. Who will buy your product?
2. Demographics - gender, age, income, education, interests, etc.
3. What do they read, watch or listen to for information?
4. What factors influence the buying decision?
5. Who is involved in the purchase decision?
6. Where do they buy?
7. How often will buyers buy?
8. Are they loyal repeat buyers?

Tip: *The 80/20 rule frequently applies to customer buying. This is where 20% of your customers provide 80% of your sales. You can dramatically grow your sales by understanding everything about this key 20% group.*

Internet Branding

Branding in Internet marketing is building the awareness of your company, products and services. Branding on the web is much more than logo, tagline, colors, graphics, image and message. It is the complete user experience on your website. It includes warm welcoming graphics, valuable information, simple intuitive navigation and easy search features. If you are selling products, it includes the layout of your store, great product photos and an easy return policy.

Familiar brand names create positive emotional responses in the brain such as safety, security, comfort and happiness. It has long been said that people shop logically, but they buy emotionally. That is why imagery, colors, and shapes are great influencers.

This applies to your Internet business. Internet branding is about creating that positive emotional response so visitors will return over and over to your website. Uncovering ways to touch your visitors at deeper emotional levels creates a stronger brand loyalty. Here are some ways to strengthen your Internet brand.

1. Identify which benefits are emotional and then how to incorporate that into your website.
2. Create ways that your Internet business can be unique, memorable and distinctive.
3. Develop a unique and emotional website design; one that makes people feel good.
4. Build trust with testimonials, guarantees and liberal return policies.
5. Be exclusive with memberships and give something of high perceived value.
6. Be Easy: Easy to search, navigate, understand and buy from.

In branding, you have to set yourself apart from everyone else in your market at an emotional, not intellectual level.

Domain Names
Your domain name is the way people will remember your website. It is part of the branding of your business. Your domain name establishes your unique identity and creates an impression on visitors to your website. You can use your domain name for your email address to create a professional business image.

1. Use your business name, product name, or keywords
2. Keep it short
3. Make it easy to remember
4. First choice is .com for a business

When possible, I like to choose the business name as the domain name. Another strong domain name is to use your product name. People instantly understand what you do and you create recognition. Using keywords in the domain name is a good strategy for getting better search engine rankings.

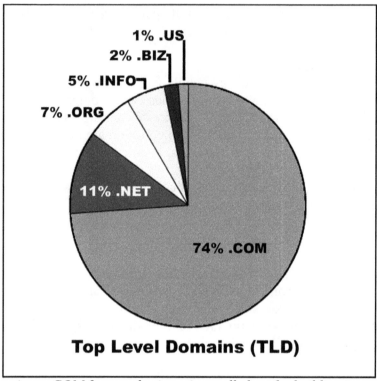

Choosing a .COM for your business is usually best for building image and customer trust. Almost 3 out of 4 domains are .COM's

Importance of color in Marketing

Have you considered the importance of color in branding? There is a powerful emotional effect caused by color. The dominant color you select for your logo, website or business blog sends a message. Choosing colors is a fundamental part of creating any design project.

According to the Institute for Color Research, people quickly make a subconscious judgment about an item and 62%-90% of that assessment is based on color alone. Judgments are based on human instincts and cultural influences and powerfully communicate.

What each color communicates

Black: Elegance, formality, mystery, death and style.
Blue: Stability, professionalism, trust, peace and coolness.
Brown: Endurance, casual, earthy, poverty and tradition.
Gray: Conservatism, seriousness and enhances messages of other colors.
Green: Safety, harmony, freshness, nature and wealth.
Orange: Enthusiasm, cheerfulness, creativity, playfulness and heat.
Pink: Hot pink: energy, youthfulness, fun and excitement... lighter pinks: sentimental, romantic.
Purple: Power, nobility, magic, sensuality and spirituality.
Red: Boldness, excitement, desire, intensity, and love.
Silver: Prestige, cold, scientific.
White: Cleanliness, purity, simplicity, peace and innocence.
Yellow: Attention-grabbing, happiness, energy, joy and optimism.

In general, red, orange, and yellow are exciting colors while purple, blue and green are calming ones. Yellow is the most visible color. Black on yellow or green on white are the most legible combination.

Many fast food restaurants are decorated with vivid reds and oranges. Studies show that these colors encourage diners to eat quickly and leave.

Combining colors in various combinations creates even different psychological effect. Now color is not the only design element to communicate with, but it is a powerful one.

It's Location, Location, Location: Eye Tracking Studies

Eye tracking studies give web designers insight into what attracts the attention of visitors. This is very important in business web design. Once you have optimized your website to bring in traffic, following a few design rules can make sure you catch your reader's attention. After all, most visitors make up their mind to stay or go in the first few seconds.

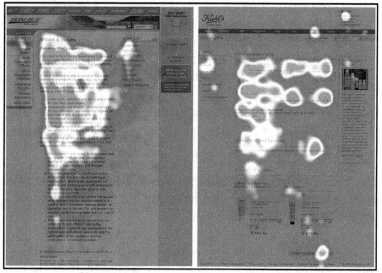

Photo courtesy of http://www.useit.com/eyetracking/. Please refer to their website for more in depth discussions on eyetracking heatmaps.

Results from the Nielsen Norman Group's study show that the dominant reading pattern looks somewhat like an "F". Web visitors begin in the upper left and sweep to the right. They then drop down the page a bit and do a shorter horizontal sweep and then they scan down the left side content.

From eye tracking studies we can establish 10 guidelines for web design.

1. Content / Images in the upper left quadrant are most likely to be seen.
2. Right side content and content lower on the page is less likely to be seen.
3. Larger font headlines draw the eye.
4. Shorter paragraphs are read more than large blocks of text.
5. Smaller font body text is read and larger font body text is scanned.
6. Numbers are read as numerals, but skipped over as text.
7. Bigger images get more attention than smaller images.
8. Bulleted or numbered lists hold readers attention.
9. Banner ads are ignored.
10. Fancy fonts and fancy words look like promotion and are ignored.

The last point was well illustrated with the U.S. Census Bureau's homepage. In a study, 86% of users failed to notice the country's current population which was presented in a large red font.

F Pattern applies to Search Results
These same eye tracking studies show that most viewers looked at results in an "F" shaped scan pattern. The eye travels vertically along the far left side of the results looking for visual cues (relevant words, brands, etc.) and then scanning to the right, as if something caught the participant's attention.

This means that top search results are read or scanned much more consistently than right side sponsored results. Sponsored Results at the top of the page and the top 5 Organic listings were noticed with a very high regularity.

These findings give high importance to organic search engine optimization and not just relying on pay per click advertising.

eCommerce Web Design

The single most important goal of an eCommerce website is getting the visitor to buy something. To do this you need to understand the psychology and marketing strategies that need to be part of your eCommerce web design.

Many of the same principles that we apply to traditional retail stores need to be applied to your eCommerce website. Make it easy to find products. A good eCommerce website design will lead the visitor to the right page in one or two clicks at most.

Plan your layout
Avoid a cluttered layout. Visual cluttering is a result of trying to put too much information onto a single page. You should limit your design to no more than 10-15 products per page and no more than 600 words of text.

Organize
Break text up into easy to read blocks or columns the way a newspaper does. Use graphics and colors to help break up the page to give a clean graphical look. Add headlines above blocks of text to allow visitors to quickly scan a page. Design a clear path for navigation to guide your visitor through your website.

Categories
Add navigation and category listings so customers can find products in different ways. Use categories like departments in your store, and sub-categories if you stock a wide variety. Allow customers to browse by price category, newest products or most popular products.

Add Search Capability
If customers have something specific in mind or know exactly what they want, allow them to search by keyword, brand, model number or a combination of these. Keep the search simple, intuitive and easy to use.

Keep the Checkout Process Simple
30-60% of customers abandon their order at checkout because of usability issues. Design your process to be 1-2 pages and only request necessary information. Use clean and organized design layouts and add a confirmation page.

E-commerce is based on trust. There are a number of other pages in the typical eCommerce website, each designed to build trust, to answer a shopper's questions and to put them at ease in doing business with you.

About Us
This is where you tell your story and tell why you are better to do business with than your competitors, what is the company's purpose, the history of your company, your philosophy of doing business. Use a creative and interesting writing style to let your potential customers get to know you. This is one of the most read pages in a website.

Testimonials
People will trust what other people say about you, much more than what you say about yourself. Positive customers that are specific are the most powerful. Here is an example of a powerful testimonial with detail. "You guys are great and helped me out of a jam; your customer service ran my order out to the airport so I could get it the same day. You're the best!"

FAQ
Frequently asked questions are an important part of the pre-sale step. By posting answers to the common questions being asked, you reduce the phone calls and emails from potential buyers. By satisfying the visitor's questions on the spot, they are much more likely to make an immediate purchase.

Privacy Policy
People are wary and want to protect their personal information. They want to know how you are going to use this information and if you will pass it onto others. This is an element in building trust.

Return Policy
One of the best ways to put customers at ease is through a well-thought-out and prominently posted returns procedure. This can range from all sales final to complete refunds.

Call to Action

A clear "call to action" is a key element of business web design and makes a difference between a website that is merely interesting and one that gets results. A "call to action" in web design refers to website content that compels a user to take action. On the web, people move quickly from site to site and look for something specific. A website that gets results has a clear focus and asks the reader to take some action. This action should be planned and designed in.

Design in what you want your visitor to do. What action should they take?

Virtually all websites have a purpose to get someone to buy, call, register, request-a-quote or subscribe. Sometimes the call to action can be less obvious, but still effective. Some examples are:

1. Watch this video and learn how to save.
2. Take our computer network security survey.
3. See examples of our business website designs.
4. Click here to see how a buying new refrigerator will pay for itself in less than one year.

In planning your website, establish the three actions you want people to do. One should be your primary call to action and the others secondary actions. Make these actions clear and precise. Organize the website navigation, page layout and even the fonts to make the primary call to action clear and easy to find.

Every time you write new web content, there should be some sort of call to action at the end of the topic. The idea is to involve the reader and encourage action.

If you would like to learn more, please go to our website and learn how your business can take advantage of our web design and Internet marketing expertise.

Testimonials Add Credibility

Effective business web marketing means breaking through this barrier in a way that adds the human touch back into the Web. Testimonials are a way of bringing in what others are saying about us. After all, what do people who have actually purchased and used your product or service think about it?

Why testimonials are important
Testimonials are important to customers because they lower the risk of doing business with an unknown company. The first hand testimony of a happy customer is more powerful than pages of

facts and figures describing the product or service. These endorsements are important because they tell your prospects and customers how others think of you.

What makes a good testimonial?
First and foremost they should be genuine and believable. They should be specific and have the person's full name and if they represent a business, the business name. Testimonials can be a comment, a review; it can be in text, audio or video.

Where to place testimonials?
Should testimonials be on their own page? Or placed around the website? We prefer to put them into a PHP Database program and do both. We will design an area on the home page where testimonial excerpts will rotate every 4-5 seconds and place these onto a testimonials page that is created from this same database.

Getting Testimonials
Testimonials should convey the biggest result your client achieved by working with you. The more specific you can be… the better. Stay away from vague generalities. They should tell about how a problem was solved, how you made them money or how you made them better.

Make requesting testimonials a part of your quality improvement process. Ask for feedback and ask for permission to publish their comments. If the feedback isn't good, use this as a tool to identify and fix problems. If the feedback is good, then you have a good marketing tool.

"Man was designed for accomplishment, engineered for success, and endowed with the seeds of greatness." - Zig Ziglar

Lead Generation

New sales leads are the lifeblood of any business. To grow your business and keep it healthy, you need a steady flow of new customers. Where will they come from? Here are 30 ways to generate new sales leads. Choose the ones that best fit your business.

1. Write a blog (see article under blog writing)
2. Add a clear call to action on your website such as "Request a Quote"
3. Optimize your website for search traffic
4. Advertise on the search engines (PPC advertising)
5. Advertise on other websites using affiliate marketing
6. Become known as an expert in your market (build trust)
7. Cold calling
8. Telemarketing
9. Direct mail or sales letters
10. Use a follow-up tool such as a post card or note card
11. Email marketing
12. Communicate using email or printed newsletters
13. Tradeshows
14. Speak regularly at business or trade events
15. Be a guest speaker on a local radio or TV show
16. Put on a seminar or workshop
17. Educational events through the telephone (teleseminars) or via the Web (webinars)
18. Write a whitepaper
19. Publish a book
20. Print advertising (newspaper, magazines, trade journals)
21. Hand out business cards at every opportunity
22. Purchase leads
23. Join a lead referral group like itakethelead.com
24. Be active in your local chamber of commerce
25. Encourage referrals from current customers
26. Encourage current customers to email questions; these are sales opportunities
27. Have good business signage to bring in drive by traffic
28. Customer complaints can, and should be treated as opportunities
29. Hire independent sales rep firm
30. Publish regular press releases

Search Engine Marketing

Your website is no different than a brick and mortar store. To be successful, you need a good location and to advertise. Search engines are the primary way that people locate information on the Internet.

Which search engines should you target? According to Hitwise (August 2007) 97% of all search volume happens on the top 4 search engines.

1. Google   64.1%
2. Yahoo   22.9%
3. MSN   6.6%
4. Ask   3.4%

Search engine marketing is aimed at increasing your website's visibility on the search engines using one or more of these three methods.
1. Search Engine Optimization
2. Pay per click
3. Paid inclusion

Search Engine Optimization or SEO focuses on increasing the amount of visitors to a web site by improving the natural or organic rankings for relevant keywords. SEO is a process for choosing and using the best keywords according to topic and search volumes. This usually involves improving link popularity and other techniques.

Pay per click: This is advertising with the search engines such as Google. You pay when someone actually clicks on an ad to visit the website. The search engines allow you to choose keywords and how much you are willing to pay. Your listings appear in the sponsored ad area alongside the other search results. They can appear as sponsored ads on participating websites.

Paid Inclusion: A payment to the search engine guarantees that your website will be included in their index. It only guarantees that your website will be spidered regularly, not any particular placement or priority. Of the 4 major search engines, only Yahoo still offers paid inclusion.

Search Engine Optimization

Search Engine Optimization or SEO is the process of improving both the volume and quality of traffic to a web site. This works with the search engines selection process to get good rankings in the organic or natural search results.

The first search engines were launched in 1994 and by 1995 the earliest SEO had its beginnings with the use of keywords. By 1997 META tag optimization was very important. In 1998 SEO was relatively easy and there was a shift toward looking at off page factors such as link popularity. Today, META Tags have very little to do with optimization and SEO has evolved into a complex science.

SEO takes hours of research, choosing the correct keywords, developing strategies to fit the company, industry and competitive environments.

Search engines sort and select data from hundreds of millions of web pages according to complex algorithms. The search engine algorithms are changing and evolving in quest of the perfect search results.

They index things such as keywords and page text which are called "on-page factors." Since on-page factors can be manipulated, search engines like Google now place much more weight on so called "off-page factors." These include links from other websites, age of a website, how many years a domain name is renewed for, how old the domain name is, etc.

Keywords are considered to be the heart of SEO. This is because all other strategies are built on top of the keywords. The wrong keywords bring lookers; the right ones bring willing buyers. Keyword selection is very important.

Business Blog Marketing

Business blogging has become a merger between social media and marketing. Blogging gets results and gets results faster than traditional Internet marketing. Businesses are quickly taking on Blog marketing as a mainstream Internet marketing strategy.

Blog marketing uses blogs to publicize or advertise a website or business. Business blog marketing is simply marketing your business using a blog. About 70% of all businesses have a website of some sort today: this is website marketing. Less than 10% of businesses today are using blogs to promote their business.

Business blogging establishes that business as an authority and is a strong branding tool. Blogging is an interactive medium that allows a business to reach out to new customers. This can include building up your company brand, building up traffic, reaching new potential clients, open communication with current customers, etc.

Blogs seem to be the magazine of the future and have become a leading presence on the Internet. Blog marketing has also become one of the best ways to learn and transmit industry news. It is estimated that in the US 27% of the people read blogs on a regular basis and this number is growing.

Blog readers tend to be early adopters and influencers. Blog readers are more likely to take an action such as calling, speaking to or emailing as a result of what they have read in a blog posting.

The marketing strategy of a business blog is similar to that of an eNewsletter. They both build credibility and an ongoing relationship with your customers and prospects. They keep your product or service first in their mind when they're ready to buy.

Email Marketing

Email marketing is a form of direct marketing as a means of reaching your targeted audience. E-mail marketing, if done correctly, can be an inexpensive and quick way to reach a large audience. The key is to get people to want to receive your mailings.

Great care must be taken not to spam in any email marketing campaign. Spam is the equivalent of unsolicited junk mail.

So where did the name spam come from? It originated from a famous Monty Python comedy skit. This was a story about a guy ordering food at a restaurant and everything on the menu was made with Spam. Spam became synonymous with unwanted stuff.

The CAN-SPAM Act of 2003 is enforced by the United States Federal Trade Commission (FTC) and establishes penalties for deceptive email advertising and requires an "opt out" mechanism for recipients in each email.

Blacklists: Anti-spam services, such as SpamCop, gathers reports about spam sources and publishes the names of those computers on a "blacklist." Mail systems will automatically reject all emails coming from that computer (and nearby computers). This disrupts email service for thousands of other users at that hosting company. For this reason, most hosting companies have developed "zero tolerance" to spam and will immediately eject a spammer and their website.

Opt-in: The key is to build-up your own mailing list with people who have given permission for you to send emails. Remember it is no longer an opt-in list if you purchase an email list and send the emails out yourself.

There are email marketing services that will send out your emails to their opt-in email lists.

By building your own opt-in mailing list, email marketing is an effective way to build a relationship using newsletters and special offers.

Email Marketing Tips

Email marketing is a great way to stay in touch with customers and interested prospects. Here are 10 tips that will help improve your response rate.

1. **Subject:** The subject is the headline. Make it concise with just 3-5 words. The subject will determine if your email will get read.
2. **Personal:** Write in a conversational tone and to an audience of one. People respond better to informal speech.
3. **Original Copy:** In the first one or two sentences make it clear why you are sending the email and grab their attention. Use original and compelling copy.
4. **Readability:** Wrap your lines at 65 characters or less. This makes for easier reading and less eye strain.
5. **Keep it short:** People on the Internet are impatient. Keep the total length under 300 words and paragraphs should be no more than 4-6 lines.
6. **Day of week:** Monday is the best response day, but Tuesday and Wednesday are very good too. Saturday and Sunday are the worst days.
7. **Unsubscribe:** Include a quick way to unsubscribe. In some countries, it's mandatory that every email has an unsubscribe link in it.
8. **Spam Filters:** To make sure your emails don't get flagged as spam, avoid using words such as "Save", "Free", "Discount" and "$$$" in the subject and body.
9. **Call-to-Action:** If you tell people what to do, they will do it. Point them in the right direction and you will improve your conversion.
10. **Website:** Use your website to complete the sale. Use the email to pique their curiosity and use the website to answer their questions.

Affiliate Marketing

Affiliate marketing uses one website to drive traffic to another. Advertisers develop a network of "affiliates" that place ads on their websites. These ads can be banners or text ads. The affiliate receives a commission each time a person clicks thru and buys a product, signs up for an offer or completes the desired action.

In affiliate marketing, the advertiser only pays for results. The affiliate partner is responsible to bring in visitors to their site. This is a pay for performance model where an affiliate is rewarded when the new client introduction results in a sale or lead. This makes it a low-risk, high-reward environment for both parties.

This form of Internet marketing is in essence a modern version of the "finder's fee" where individuals are rewarded for business referrals.

Affiliate programs can be managed in-house or through independent networks. Larger independent networks like Linkshare or Commission Junction will give almost instant recruitment and faster establishment of your network. In-house management can give you more control and the ability to make faster adjustments to get the results that you need.

Examples
Started in 1996, Amazon.com is one of the oldest affiliate marketers on the Internet. Website owners register with Amazon and place advertising on their sites. When visitors click through on these ads and purchase a book or other product, the web site owner is paid a commission for generating the sale.

Google Adsense was launched in 2003. This form of affiliate marketing offers web sites a way to generate revenue through placement of targeted ads (from Google Adwords) adjacent to their content.

Viral Marketing

Viral marketing is sometimes referred to as "word-of-mouth marketing" or "network marketing." This uses social networks to carry a message, an idea or a brand name across the Internet. They take on a life of their own and like viruses, replicate and multiply. They can take the form of a funny video clip, images or a Flash game.

Hotmail is a classic example of a successful viral marketing campaign. In its first 18 months, they signed up 12 million subscribers for free email service. They did this with a marketing budget of only $500,000. If you run the math, this is less than 5 cents per subscriber. Juno went after the same market and ended up spending almost $5 per subscriber and ended up with one-third of the users.

How did Hotmail do it?
1. They gave away free e-mail addresses and services.
2. On the bottom of each and every email was the phrase, "Get your free private email at www.hotmail.com."
3. Users send this offer along with their emails.
4. Their friends and associates sign-up.
5. This grows exponentially as it is taken into wider and wider groups and circles.

Viral marketing programs give something of value away for free. This can be an email account, an e-Book, free software or free information. "Cheap" will attract attention and generate interest… but not as much or as fast as "Free."

To be effective, a viral marketing incentive must be quickly scalable from a low volume to an extremely high volume. Downloadable incentives are very easy to scale up or down with demand.

Podcast Marketing

Podcast marketing is one of the newest marketing frontiers with its beginnings in 2004. It is newer than blog marketing. The term "podcast" was first used in a February 2004 article by Ben Hammersley who coined the term podcast to mean audio blogging or amateur internet radio.

Podcasting moved beyond audio blogging and it is now an audio or video that can be downloaded to a portable MP3 player, or viewed on a PC.

This is targeted digital broadcasting, where people choose to listen to your message. MP3 players are now being integrated into cell phones. 2007 forecasted sales for MP3 players are 120 million and 200 million for MP3 enabled cell phones.

Podcasting allows listeners to listen to what they want, when they want and where they want. Choices for topics are unlimited. It is ideal for listeners who want new, interesting and plentiful content to fill their MP3 players.

Now you can target a specific niche market with your message. Broadcasting to a small audience may not seem cost effective… but this small audience has chosen to listen to your message. Targeting the correct market with an interesting message can achieve a very high conversion rate of listeners to customers.

Use podcasting along with other Internet marketing strategies such as blogging and website marketing. Consider adding a podcast library to your website.

Designing a podcast
1. Determine the marketing opportunity
2. Identify the target audience
3. Develop a central message

4. Choose keyword phrases
5. Select your format (Interview, call-in, guest, expert, etc.)
6. Distribution plan (blog, network)
7. Write your script in a conversational tone
8. Write a written summary with keywords
9. Produce and publish

"A market is never saturated with a good product, but it is very quickly saturated with a bad one." – Henry Ford

Chapter 5 Blog Marketing Strategies

Before you begin blogging, you need to build your own blog marketing strategy. You should begin by answering some questions about what you want to accomplish.

What is the most important thing to accomplish? This can include building up your company brand, building up traffic to the blog, reaching new potential clients, open communication with current customers, etc. You may want to create a list and then choose the most important.

List two more objectives that are important to you. This will give you a total of three objectives. More than three objectives total are too difficult to focus on. Most of the activity should be on accomplishing the most important objective.

Who would want to read your blog? This is your targeted audience. This should be the same as your targeted customer if one of your objectives is to increase sales.

How much time can you commit? To reach your objectives you will need to commit writing resources. This will either mean your time or one of your employees.

How much money have you budgeted? Set up a marketing budget for site design, videos, ghost writers, etc.

Example
Objective: Build blog traffic to 500 unique visitors each day.
Strategies/Tactics:
Write new and original content about...
Engage readers emotionally in each post.
Commenting on at least 5 industry and local blogs.

Allergy and Asthma Clinic

Local 3 physician medical clinic specializing in Allergy and Asthma disorders

Objectives: Improve the search rankings of clinic website to be better found by local visitors. Secondary objectives are to brand the clinic as an expert authority and to build visitor traffic up to the blog.

Targeting: Target people looking for allergy and asthma information, treatments and news.

Tactics

1. **Increase website size**: Add the blog as part of current clinic website to add relevant content and provide resource materials for patients and interested visitors. This will act as "spider food" for the search engines.
2. **Keywords**: People search most often for "allergy relief" or for specific types of allergies. Use these phrases in the titles, link text and content of each blog posting. Use these keywords plus local city and community names on each of the static pages of the website to help bring in local visitor traffic.
3. **Content**: Provide riveting reading about how people are diagnosed, treated and sometimes cured. Include discussions of new methods and strategies for treating and managing all types of allergic disorders. Ideas for topics and categories include Food Allergies, Diagnostics and Treatments, Dust Mites, Hay Fever, Mold Allergies, Pet Allergies, Living with Allergies, Product reviews, Allergy Tips and Laws and legislation.
4. **Video**: Use video clips to attract visitors and to be different than other allergy blogs.
5. **Branding**: Present as the knowledgeable authority on allergies and asthma through our blog postings so prospective patients will contact us for treatment and consultation. Use understandable everyday language.

Boutique Clothing Store

This is a women's upscale retail boutique with 4 store locations and Internet sales. Products include upscale boutique fashions, brand name women's clothing, jewelry and accessories

Objectives: To brand the company as a leading fashion expert and consultant. To develop a large loyal readership and to use the blog to improve the search engine rankings of the primary company website. Long-term objectives include franchising in other metropolitan areas.

Targeting: Nationwide readership of fashion conscious middle to upper income women in the 20-45 age range.

Tactics
1. **Looks are everything:** Fashion is the business of making people look good. The blog and its postings need to reflect that. Organization, colors, layout are critical in establishing the brand. Use clear product photos in every posting.
2. **Topic ideas:** Be a continual source of fashion help with postings on fashion tips, how to articles, newest trends, celebrity fashions, style on a budget, fashion rules, seasonal ideas, accessorizing and makeover ideas.
3. **Emotional appeal:** Postings need to be passionate to connect with the reader at a deeper emotional level and to encourage action. Buying boutique quality is more an emotional purchase than a logical one.
4. **Trend Setter:** As a fashion leader and expert, express clear opinions. The goal is to teach and not just report information. Creating some controversy is a good way to establish the company name in the consumers' minds.
5. **Search Engines:** SEO is built around "designer clothing"

deep linking to the store at the primary website. Use brand names and descriptions in link text to bring in search engine traffic.

Dollhouse Miniatures eCommerce Store

Miniature dollhouse furniture and dollhouse kits sold thru Internet sales

Objectives: To build up targeted visitor traffic to 200 unique targeted visitors per day within 3 months, brand the website as an expert and improve Search Engine Rankings.

Targeting: The primary targeted group would be women in the age range of 30-60. This would be people that are interested in the hobby of building dollhouses for themselves or as a family project.

Tactics
1. **Blog**: The blog will be located as part of the main website and not on a separate domain. The blog will be the primary source of relevant content for the search engines.
2. **Content:** Regularly write interesting articles on putting together dollhouses. Include tips and how to articles with decorating and customizing ideas. The idea is to bring new people into the hobby and help those just beginning. Create new market opportunities by writing about "non-hobby" uses of dollhouse building such as crime scene reconstructions, tradeshow displays, model home displays and models for the interior designer.
3. **Photos:** Use product photos in every posting to generate interest and help readers visualize the realism of the miniature furniture.
4. **Comments**: Regularly read other related blogs and leave comments that have a link back to your blog. Use this as a way of bringing in referral traffic and creating links back to the website for search optimization.

5. **Brand as Expert:** Make entry into this hobby easy by providing great resource materials and information for visitors. Use the blog postings to create an eBook about decorating dollhouses.
6. **Linking:** Each posting will have at least one link back to a specific product page that is highly relevant to the posting.

Fishing Guide Service

Columbia River area fishing guide

Objective: First is to get the phone ringing. Very few people will actually sign up for a fishing trip without a phone conversation. Branding as the expert on local fishing and increasing traffic directly to the website are secondary goals.

Targeting: Looking for groups of people that want a quality fishing experience with all the equipment supplied. This includes tourists traveling to the area and businesses wanting to book trips with valued clients and prospective clients.

Tactics
1. **Fishing Reports:** People interested in local fishing search for up-to-date fishing reports. Use the blog to put out daily updates on local fishing. Discuss where the fishing is hot and when the various seasons are going to open and close.
2. **Locate on Website:** Add the blog as part of the main website to bring in visitor traffic. This adds new relevant content into the website for search optimization.
3. **Expert Branding:** By maintaining information on local fishing conditions, this guide service will be viewed as the expert on where to catch fish. Become the natural choice as the guide service to hire.
4. **Locate Fishing Updates:** In addition to the information network that the guide service has, add a feed reader to the guide's computer and subscribe to all the regional fishing reports available including the fish and wildlife service.

5. **Search Rankings:** Regular postings with locations and fish species will add keyword rich content for search engine positioning.
6. **Lead Generation:** The phone number and booking form will be located on every page of the blog.

Flight Attendant Training

School that provides training for flight attendant careers

Objectives: To obtain inquiries from people who would like a career as a Flight Attendant. Secondary objectives include improving the rankings of the school's website and to brand the school as the premier training center for flight attendants.

Targeting: Target young adult women and men who are interested in an exciting career in the travel industry.

Tactics
1. **Content:** Include actual stories from flight attendants from real life situations to show why it is a great career. This can include meeting famous people, memorable experiences, advice and tips and even just normal routine days.
2. **Writing Style:** Keep all the stories real and being told in the first person by the person. The idea is to give people insight into what this career is really like.
3. **Search Engine Optimization:** Focus on the keywords "flight attendant school" and "flight attendant career" in the blog content, titles and links. Use an off-site blog to maximize the link popularity benefit to the main website.
4. **Lead Generation:** Include a link to an inquiry form to capture people interested in career training.
5. **Branding:** Writing good and interesting blog postings will build up a repeat readership. This will also build a reputation for the school as the flight attendant training experts.
6. **Request for Stories:** Encourage readers that are flight

attendants to send in their own stories. These stories, if they are good, will be used in future blogs. This can help create an industry wide excitement about this blog.

Golf Products – eCommerce

Online store that sells golf bags, clubs, carts, shoes, accessories, books and videos

Objectives: Brand the company as a "golf expert". Build a reputation as a quality resource for "how to" improve your golf game with the "store" being the stock of solutions that the readers are looking for. Use the blog to build search engine rankings for the main website.

Targeting: Readers are projected to be 70% male with a high disposable income. They will be professionals, semi retired or retired that play lots of golf.

Tactics

1. **Quality image**: The look and layout of the blog needs to be organized, upper end and high quality to appeal to the targeted audience.
2. **Content**: Provide content that hits points that golfers are interested in. Provide a good balance of text and graphics to maintain reader attention. Keep it entertaining and informative. Use video clips from time to time.
3. **Write reviews**: Present product reviews and link to them. Throughout postings, mention products in passing, write articles or tips and recommend products.
4. **Topics**: Write about golfing techniques, golf psychology, latest news and tips on how to improve their game. Provide a link to a product that most closely fits that topic.

Selling will be done at a very low key level.

5. **Search Engine Optimization**: Links back to the main website will be both structurally in the blog navigation and in the posting itself. Use "make and model" link text since that is what golf equipment buyers tend to search by.

Home Improvement Online Retailer

Online retailer for the do-it-yourself home improvement market

Objective: Increase rankings and visitor traffic for the primary company website.

Targeting: Target homeowners who want to remodel, improve and decorate their homes. For do-it-yourselfers that are taking on larger projects.

Tactics
1. **Keywords**: Focus on general home improvement phrases of "home improvement diy" which has 255 searches per day on Google and "kitchen remodel" which has 1,179 searches per day on Google.
2. **Blog Format**: Use XHTML-CSS blog template customized to take on the look of the primary website. The blog will be hosted on a separate domain and server from the company websites to maximize the link popularity benefits.
3. **Linking Plan**: Develop a large volume of one-way blog links. Use the targeted phrases in the content link text and deep link into the main website.
4. **Categories**: Focus on projects and make use of keyword phrases; so we will use Home Improvement-DIY, Kitchen remodel, bathroom remodel, basement remodel, etc.
5. **Content**: Provide tips, methods, material lists and tutorials that will be helpful to the do it yourself homeowner. The idea is for this blog to become a great resource for the homeowner and give great ideas with links to the products

and tools that will get the job done.
6. **Video**: Add regular 60-90 second videos into the blog postings to stand out from the other blogs (branding) and to add interest (build-up readership).
7. **Branding**: Brand the company as the expert resource for home improvement projects. Make it easy for readers to locate and buy the materials required in the projects described.

Lawyer Blog (Blawg)

Nationwide law practice that specializes in Paxil related cases

Objectives:
1. Brand law firm as an expert in Paxil litigation.
2. Create a base of loyal readers.
3. Improve search positions on Google and other engines.

Targeting: Families who have lost babies after the pregnant mother took Paxil and people who suffered extreme symptoms of withdrawal when trying to stop taking the drug.

Tactics
1. **Interesting Content**: Provide valuable content focused on Paxil including updates on class action lawsuit, information on the drug and its effects, late breaking announcements and other closely related news. Provide commentaries and tips for people curious about pursuing a claim. Blogs that track a particular area of law are more likely to be read regularly than the more general blogs.
2. **Expert Status:** Regularly publish up-to-date content about the area of Paxil litigation and become the law firm of choice for both would be clients and referrals from other attorneys. Blogs are generally effective in improving the reputation of lawyers among Internet users.
3. **Create Relationship**: By targeting our potential client base with information, we are able to engage them with regular

information and engage them in discussions through comments. Blogs are an effective means of face-to-face conversation with a client or prospect when you can't meet them face-to-face.

4. **Build Referral Base**: Be an active reader of other blawgs – link, comment, reference others, even the competition. Use this as a networking tool with other attorneys.
5. **Search Positions**: Optimize each blog post with the targeted keyword phrase of paxil lawyer. Host the blog offsite to create one-way links to the site in each post made.

Residential Mortgage Financing

Full service residential mortgage company with offices in Akron, Cincinnati, Columbus, and Dayton

Objectives: The ultimate purpose of this blog is to increase the number of mortgage leads from the Ohio area. Secondary objectives include being branded as the residential mortgage specialist and increasing traffic to the primary company website.

Targeting: Target people who are planning and budgeting to purchase a home or refinance a current home. Real estate agents who will recommend a mortgage loan company to their clients.

Tactics
1. **Lead Generation:** Give a reason for readers to willingly supply their email address or phone number. Embed a "Fast-Quote" form on every page of the blog with a promise of a customized rate quote with a pre-qualification letter within two business hours.
2. **Content:** Build up a local readership by posting articles about local home sales, mortgage rate projections, economic news, ways to qualify for the best rates and tips on raising your credit score. Include the latest financial rates on the blog sidebar so Realtors will bookmark and return to the blog regularly.

3. **Branding:** Writing good blog postings is similar to being active in community organizations. Being helpful and building relationships builds business referrals. Build a reputation as the mortgage experts in the Ohio area that can get the best rates and close loans with a minimum of hassle.
4. **Search Engine Optimization:** Focus on the keywords "Ohio mortgage rates" and "Ohio mortgage lenders" in the blog content, titles and links. These phrases will be combined with local community names to help bring in local searches and interest. Use an off-site blog to maximize the link popularity benefit to the main website.

Residential Real Estate Appraiser

Values local real estate properties for bank loans, estates and divorces

Objectives: Build a readership of people interested in local real estate pricing trends and statistics. Secondary objectives are branding the appraiser company as the local expert on real estate pricing and search engine optimization of the business website.

Targeting: Target people who are interested in local residential real estate pricing, trends and growth. This will include: (1) People buying, selling and relocating to this area. (2) People interested in valuation for estates and divorces. (3) Local real estate professionals that want up-to-date info for their clients.

Tactics
1. **Blog location:** Locate the blog as part of main website to add keyword rich content and provide resource materials for prospects and interested visitors. This will act as "spider food" for the search engines.
2. **Content**: Publish valuation trends, statistics and graphs for local communities that are available from special appraiser resources. Use of local town names and neighborhood names will help bring in local searches.

3. **Branding**: Brand as the local real estate valuation expert. Want to be the source of info for real estate sales people who are blogging.
4. **Keywords**: Focus on the keyword phrases real estate appraisal, real estate appraiser and residential appraisals. These phrases will be combined with local community names to create an array of phrases and bring in search engine traffic.
5. **Networking**: Encourage local real estate blogs and mortgage blogs to link to the appraisal blog and in return include them on the site's Blogroll. This will create a network of local real estate resources for visitors and will also help with search engine rankings.

Residential Real Estate Sales

Objectives: Brand yourself as the local Real Estate expert, build up visitor traffic, and search engine optimization of primary website.

Targeting: Current home owners who want to sell and purchase new homes, new home buyers, people wanting to relocate and out of area Realtors who may have referrals. Build readership in the local metro area.

Tactics
1. **Build-up readership:** Do this by writing interesting quality postings about local Real Estate issues. Discuss local market conditions, write "how to" tutorials such as how to stage your house, where the best deals are, give insights into upcoming zoning changes, comment on how national trends are affecting the local market, trends in local housing starts, etc. The bottom line is to keep a local perspective.
2. **Video:** Add regular 60-90 second videos into the blog postings to stand out from the other blogs (branding) and to add interest (build-up readership).

3. **Branding**: Brand yourself as the knowledgeable Real estate expert. Do this by writing about the local area with very interesting and timely postings. Give advice, ideas and offer real helpful advice. Not only do you become a local real estate expert and increase your search engine positioning but your visitors will keep coming back to your site time and time again.

4. **Search Engine Optimization**: Focus on no more than 3 keyword phrases. Combine these with local areas such as city, county, area names and neighborhood names. It is the local names that will bring in the local traffic. Use keyword phrases in link text and deep link to the primary website. The link text is extremely important to search engines such as Google.

Retail Jewelry Store plus Internet Sales

Fashion Jewelry for Men and Women. Designer produces jewelry from natural materials and markets from a single retail location and is expanding into Internet sales. Fashion jewelry for men and women includes earrings, bracelets, chokers, anklets and necklaces

Objectives: The primary objective is getting excellent search rankings and sales for the eCommerce jewelry website. Other objectives include to build brand loyalty; brand the company as the expert in jewelry fashion and to build traffic to the blog.

Targeting: The primary buyer tends to be women in the 20-40 age range. Target consumers looking for help on buying jewelry, the latest fashion trends and help making choices in selecting jewelry.

Tactics
1. **Offsite Blog:** This will allow the blog to be viewed as an independent resource.
2. **Keywords**: People most often search by types of jewelry.

Examples include: men's, women's, bracelets, necklaces, gold, silver, natural, diamond, gemstone.

3. **Linking**: Deep link using keywords in the link text. Link directly into the ecommerce store.

4. **Content**: Write content that presents fashion ideas for the targeted audience. This will include ideas on how to accessorize using jewelry, how to identify quality in jewelry, trends in design and fashion, how celebrities are using jewelry, to accessories fashion and shopping tips for men when buying women's jewelry.

5. **Photos**: Include photos and graphics to grab the reader's attention. Jewelry is a visual product.

6. **Branding:** Brand as a fashion accessory expert and a trend setter. Express clear opinions and do not be afraid to create some controversy. The idea is to get people talking.

Specialty Financing Company

Lump sum payments for structured settlements and annuities

Objectives: Improve the natural search rankings of primary website and to generate leads. Brand the company as an expert at helping people.

Targeting: People who have received structured settlements as a result of a lawsuit or personal injury. People who are receiving payments over time in the form of an annuity where they want to convert this into a lump sum payment.

Tactics
1. **Content:** Write interesting posts about how a lump sum payout works, current news and legislation, what to look for in a lump sum payout company, what to avoid and tax implications.

2. **Cases Studies:** At least once a week present a real story (names and location changed) of how a person's life has

been helped with a lump sum payout.
3. **Writing Style:** Most financial type blogs are written in a dry impersonal style. Postings need to be written at a deeper more emotional level to encourage action.
4. **Lead Generation:** Directly link to the quote request form from every blog page. Make it easy for someone who reads an interesting blog posting to request more information.
5. **Keywords:** Focus on only two keyword phrases of "sell annuities" and "structured settlements." This is a highly competitive area so this will be a much focused writing campaign.
6. **Linking:** The blog is being located on a separate domain and on a separate server so that each link will be a more valued one-way link. Keywords will be used in the link text and links will be to highly relevant interior pages on the main website.

Steel Buildings Manufacturer

Sales of metal and steel building systems for commercial, farm and residential

Objectives: The buying cycle for steel buildings is long. Engage readers that are in the research phase, develop relationships and educate them on the advantages of your buildings. Brand the company as the best in quality and value. Use the blog to improve search rankings of the primary website. Encourage quote requests.

Targeting: Owners and Managers typically make the buying decisions or recommendations. Those that spend time researching major building purchases.

Tactics
1. **Content**: Encourage repeat visitor traffic by publishing interesting postings. Topic ideas include the advantages of steel buildings, specific uses and design ideas, the design/building process, tips on what to avoid, what

features makes a quality steel building, what warranties should you look for, etc.

2. **Photos**: Most blogs in this industry do not seem to publish. Use photos as examples and to help differentiate this blog.
3. **Branding:** Use quality as the basis for all discussions, content and look of the blog.
4. **Quote Request:** Add a link on every blog page to the request quote form on the company website.
5. **Search Engine Optimization:** Use a focused keyword strategy. Each posting will use the phrase "steel buildings" as the core phrase. The blog is located on a separate domain and on a separate server so links back to the main website will be highly valued one-way links.
6. **Deep Linking**: Every posting (where appropriate) will have a link directly to a specific products page such as "church steel buildings" or "commercial steel warehouses."

Vacation Rental Property Management

Company rents and manages vacation rentals for owners. Located in a popular vacation destination, these rentals are in three separate nearby cities

Objectives: Brand the blog as the premier information resource for the local area. Promote the activities and fun that can be had in the area. Promote the available rentals and improve search engine rankings. People research an area prior to booking a vacation rental.

Targeting: People that are interested in events, restaurants and the local area.

Tactics
1. **Create a community blog:** Set up a feed reader to

subscribe to 25-50 very local blogs that at least occasionally discuss upcoming events, local activities (fishing, golf, shopping), restaurant reviews and local news. This creates a regular resource stream of local happenings. Each day, choose one or two of the most interesting postings and write a paragraph on each with links back to the original posting.

2. **Local Events:** Use upcoming events to create interest and encourage bookings of rentals.
3. **Include photos:** Photos and graphics are great reader attention magnets.
4. **Videos:** Add in video clips of local area, events, etc. Pull from YouTube.com and other video websites; give link and acknowledgement to original source.
5. **Promote Rentals:** Link to 2-3 individual listings at the bottom of each posting that are featured or just the closest to the featured topic or event. This is also a good deep linking strategy for SEO.
6. **Search Engine Optimization:** Focus on no more than 3 keyword phrases. Link these phrases back to the company website at least once in each posting. Use city names in category names and link text since people use city names in their searches.

"Half the money I spend on advertising is wasted, and the problem is I do not know which half. " - Lord Leverhulme 1851-1925

Chapter 6 Your Digital Reputation

Web 2.0 and blogging is changing our world on how we do business. Your online reputation or digital reputation is your credibility in cyberspace. Businesses today need to monitor what is being said about them not only on the Internet, but also out in the blogosphere.

Digital reputations can be made or lost quickly. Disgruntled customers have access to online publishing tools equipped with RSS and can quickly spread their story. Just as powerfully, good stories of extraordinary customer service can quickly build a positive digital reputation.

Marketing departments use PR to build the traditional reputation for a company and its brands. The blogosphere adds a new dimension to business marketing. These new tools greatly increase the speed in building or destroying a brand.

Companies Internet marketing and blog marketing strategies should include monitoring the Blogosphere and Internet for what is being said about your company, your brands and your competitors. This is one of the costs of doing business in today's world, especially if you are a public facing company where image is an important asset.

Protect Your Online Reputation
1. Set up strategies to monitor blogosphere and the Internet using Google Alerts and Technorati. Or you can use paid services to do this monitoring for you.
2. Create an optimized website and blog that will allow you to rise above any negative buzz that may be said.
3. Have a plan in advance on how you will react to negative comments or events.

Managing Your Digital Reputation

Having to watch and manage your online reputation is sometimes thought of as the dark side of Web 2.0. Reputation monitoring and management have become a way of life for celebrities, public officials, major companies and all sorts of web related businesses.

Bad news just travels faster than good news. A bad online reputation can negatively affect sales, customer relations, brand names, employee retention, friendships and even families. With over 70% of the population online today and well over 90% of businesses making use of the Internet, a good online reputation is crucial for business.

Today, reputation management is becoming important to even the average person. 40% of the companies responding to a survey replied that they always or sometimes used Google or another search engine to research or learn more about a prospective hire. This means managing your own digital reputation is becoming increasingly important for those seeking key positions.

Managing your online reputation has 3 levels. Hopefully, you won't need to move beyond the first level.
1. **Monitoring the blogosphere**: Set-up tracking systems to notify as soon as a posting is made anywhere about yourself, your company or your brand name. If you were going to use only a single tool, then Google Alerts would be the most comprehensive.
2. **Responding to criticism - damage control**: Once you detect a problem, it is important to determine the best response (if any) to minimize the damage or perhaps turn around someone who is a foe, into an advocate.
3. **Reputation repair**: Once damage is done there is a process you need to follow to repair and restore your reputation.

Since you can't remove what was written (in some cases it is possible) you have to use a campaign of positive PR that focuses on your targeted keyword (usually your name) to dilute and push the negative comments deeper into the search results.

Monitoring the Blogosphere

What are people saying about you? Is your business being talked about on blogs? What is being said? Is this something you need to address before it gets out of control? Monitoring the blogosphere has become a cost of being a part of the Internet world that we live in today.

Businesses need to be proactive about managing their digital reputation. In addition to monitoring what is being said about your company and its brands, it's necessary to know what's being said about your competitors. This can put you ahead and potentially into new opportunities.

You can track what is being said yourself, but that takes time. You can hire another company, but that takes more money. Monitoring blog conversations can be done using tools available on the internet whether you choose to do this yourself or hire someone else.

Here are seven great blog monitoring tools:
1. Monitor News feeds with Yahoo News or Google News.
2. Search blog results only using Google Blog search (blogsearch.google.com).
3. Technorati has many advanced blog search capabilities.
4. Be emailed alerts anytime your company name or brand name is detected by Google on the Internet with Google Alerts (google.com/alerts). This alert can be set to by source type (blogs, web, news, all, etc).

5. Search forums or create alerts with boardtracker.com.
6. Monitor blog conversations and which other blogs link to a blog conversation with the BlogPulse conversation tracker (blogpulse.com/conversation).
7. Watch trends in how often your company name or brand is used with the BlogPulse trend tool (blogpulse.com/trend).

By combining several of these tools, you can get a good idea of who is talking about you, your company or your competition.

Responding to Criticism

OK, you are monitoring the blogosphere and someone has just slammed your company or your brand in a blog. How do you handle this? There are no hard and fast rules, but here are some guidelines to follow.

1. **Wait and Watch:** Take a little time to watch and gauge the reaction. Jumping in and confronting the situation can take someone's comments who is just blowing off steam and create a major controversy. If no one is paying attention or commenting, it may be best to let the person vent and then die out on its own. Bloggers quickly move on to new stories that grab their attention.
2. **Avoid Rebuttals:** A negative review of your product should not bring a strong response. Refuting or directly attacking the blogger will bring others to their defense and inflame the situation. Don't try and take a strong position and intimidate or bully the blogger.
3. **Be concerned and helpful:** You are entering as a guest on a blog so show respect; you will likely get respect in return. Avoid sarcasm and try to be genuine and helpful. A negative review should be treated as constructive criticism. Offer to help resolve the issue and listen to the complaints.

How you handle the situation can convert a foe into a friend.

4. **Be Impartial.** Stay away from opinions and arguments. Use objective information and if possible, third party data and statistics to show your point. Links to sites other than your own can be good convincers.
5. **Follow Thru:** If you make promises and commitments, follow thru on what you have promised.

The key in dealing with situations in the blogosphere is to listen and respond honestly in a helpful manner. This can go a long way in diffusing an explosive situation.

10 Step Process for Online Reputation Repair

No matter how good and honest you or your company is; accusations of misconduct can quickly damage your online digital reputation. You may not be able to erase what has been said, but there are steps you can take to minimize the damage. The goal should be to push the damaging statements down in the organic search results and replace these with positive information.

1. **Research**: Look at the root cause of the online discussions and what can be done to bring the conversations to an end. The repair process can only start once the controversy ends.
2. **Keywords**: Settle on the targeted phrases. Keep the focus to one phrase or two at the most. This could be your name, company, brand or an event.
3. **Identify**: List out articles, websites and blogs that already exist that should be moved to displace the damaging stories.
4. **Your Website**: Add new material and fully optimize the primary website for the company, brand or celebrity. This is the one website that you completely control.

5. **Link Popularity**: Launch linking campaigns for the identified articles, blogs, etc. that you want to be found. Use the keyword phrases in the link text for the best results.

6. **Blogging and Press Releases**: Launch one or more blogs where you can control the content. Use independent blog networks and have blogs written based on press release. Release traditional press releases through normal media channels.

7. **Wikipedia**: For people or companies with prominent reputations, this is a key resource. If an article exists, add content and make changes. If none exists, consider starting a new topic.

8. **YouTube and Flickr**: Promote and publish videos and photos. Title them and tag them with your targeted keyword phrase.

9. **Monitor and do damage control**: Monitor the blogosphere for negative or disparaging remarks. Address these quickly and appropriately.

10. **Measure results:** Monitor the first 3 pages of the search results for Google, Yahoo and MSN. Record the positions of the articles you want to purge. You are successful when they no longer appear in the first 3 pages of results.

Monitoring for Market Intelligence

The blogosphere is made up of hundreds of millions of blog postings that reflect all aspects of life and business. This huge pool of information is searchable using blog search engines. Information can be retrieved automatically every time a brand name or keyword is used using Google Alerts.

Businesses are using the blogosphere for marketing intelligence. Companies are monitoring the public buzz. They listen to what their customers are saying, what their competitors are saying and what new directions their market is heading. If your company is

120

not listening to what is being said, you are missing out on an important source for market intelligence.

About You: Discussions take place in real time. These include discussions about your brand and customer perceptions. Before establishing a blog presence, Dell used common tools such as de.licio.us and Technorati to monitor customer perceptions. They then launched their own blog (direct2dell.com) to address issues.

Customers: From your customers you can learn what directions they are taking their business. You can learn the challenges they are facing which may mean opportunities for your business. What are their motivations and how do they make their buying decisions?

Competitors: From your competitors you can learn what new directions or technologies they are considering. Listen to what your competitor's customers are saying. Are they satisfied or are they ready to make a change? Monitoring your competitors press releases can give access to breaking news and research.

Market: The blogosphere is full of conversations about every conceivable market and industry. Is your market changing with some new technology that is being adopted? Learn about factors, concerns and excitement that are affecting the long-term growth rate of your industry.

The blogosphere is full of information and speculation that can open new opportunities if you are willing to listen. Keep an eye on your most direct competition or even more importantly, their largest customers to give you a leading indicator of change. Use blogs as a way to listen to and involve customers.

"It takes many good deeds to build a good reputation, and only one bad one to lose it"-- Benjamin Franklin quotes

Biz Blog Marketing

Chapter 7 Legal Side of Blogging

The Internet may still feel something like the Wild West, but there are US laws being enacted and interpreted that affect its use. This chapter of the book looks at some of those that affect businesses using blogging as a marketing tool. In business blog marketing, it is important to understand the legal landscape.

Disclaimer: *This chapter deals with laws that affect blogging and the Internet. It is written and published by non-legal professionals to be informative and educational. It does not provide specific legal advice nor is it intended to create an attorney client relationship. The information should not be used as a substitute for competent legal advice from a licensed professional attorney.*

If you're concerned about the legal ramifications of anything related to blogging, consulting an actual attorney with expertise in such matters would be wise.

Should You Allow Blog Comments?

Does allowing comments to be made on your blog create a legal liability? Should you turn off the ability for comments? Does moderating or editing comments increase your legal exposure? The ability for visitors to interact and comment on a blog posting is at the heart of blogging and Web 2.0.

These are questions that have been creating lively debates in the blogging community. Some risk adverse bloggers have stopped allowing comments on their blogs because of this.

There have been a number of suits brought forth in US District Courts in recent years. These suits have dealt with Section 230 (of the Communications Decency Act). The results of these cases indicate that web publishers cannot be sued for libel based on comments posted on their websites.

It appears that there is little reason for a blog owner to worry about comments made by others. You can't be treated as if you were the speaker just because you provided the platform for the libel. Even if you moderate or edit the comments, you are protected as long as you do not change the meaning or add libelous statements yourself.

Even though Section 230 does not require a blog owner take down malicious comments, it is probably wise to do so once notified. Acting in good faith to avoid conflict is better than escalating a conflict.

The Internet is global and different countries have different laws. If the person being libeled is in another country other laws may apply.

What does this mean?
1. Use good judgment on accepting or removing potentially libelous comments.
2. In your terms of use statement, disclose that you will

disapprove, moderate or edit comments if they appear libelous.

This article was not written by a lawyer and it does not intend to constitute legal advice.

Is Deep Linking Legal?

Deep linking involves linking from a blog or website to an inside page of another website instead of to the home page. One of the conventions in blogging is for writers to link to any published document on another blog or website. This is an easy way for readers to get additional information on a subject.

Some website owners object to deep links into their content. This is because linking bypasses the advertising on their main pages. If these sites are supported by advertising, this deep linking bypasses the sponsors of the website. Readers may also be confused as to who created the content.

In a 2002 ruling, US District Judge Harry Hupp declared that such "Hyperlinking does not itself involve a violation of the Copyright Act." This was a case in which involved Tickets.com against Ticketmaster.

In Europe, the court decisions have been inconsistent. In Germany, Mainpost sued NewsClub, a news headline aggregator, over deep linking. However, the court declared such linking to be legal and stressed the importance of deep links for the internet.

In Denmark, an opposite ruling occurred. The Bailiff's Court of Copenhagen ruled in favor of the Danish Newspaper Publishers Association which claimed that Danish company Newsbooster violated copyright laws by "deep linking" to newspaper articles. This was because the two companies were found to be in direct competition with each other.

124

So far, courts have found that deep links to web pages were neither a copyright infringement nor a trespass.

What does this mean?
1. You shouldn't claim that a page or file is your work unless it actually is.
2. Deep linking is an established blogging practice and you are probably fine in linking to other bloggers or to newspapers.

This article was not written by a lawyer and it does not intend to constitute legal advice.

Authenticity in Product Reviews

The practice of "Astroturfing" or producing a fake grassroots campaign is coming under scrutiny. This applies to fake blogs or fake product reviews in an effort to sway public and consumer opinion.

Paid posts for writing product reviews have become common in the blogging community. Companies hire people to either write blog reviews that are favorable or to place favorable comments on other blogs.

Most companies take an ethical approach and compensate bloggers for both good and bad reviews.
Jeremy Toeman states "As an example, at Sling Media I implemented a strict policy that no employee was to add comments about the Slingbox on any blog or review site (such as CNET or Amazon) without disclosing their employment status."

We are now seeing laws and regulations being created and enforced to protect consumers.

The Times of London has reported that the European Union is expected to overhaul its consumer laws by early 2008. They will make it "a crime to falsely represent oneself as a consumer on blogs or other online forums."

The US Federal Trade Commission (section 5 of the FTC act) deals with failure to disclose that a marketer is paying a sponsored consumer to make claims to other consumers about the marketer's product.

The key is that when a connection exists between the endorser and the seller of a product that significantly affects the endorsement, such connection must be fully disclosed.

What does this mean?
1. Bloggers should never claim to be an objective and unbiased source if they are not.
2. Bloggers should disclose posts that are paid reviews.

This article was not written by a lawyer and it does not intend to constitute legal advice.

Blogging and Copyright Issues

When you write your own blog, you are creating a copyright protected work. When you use other people's work always assume that it is likewise protected, until you are able to confirm otherwise.

Copyright is a form of protection provided by the laws of the United States. Copyright protects written, creative or artistic works. For blogs and website content, this includes images, videos, website content and even programming code. Copyright only protects the actual work itself, not the idea or concept behind it. A person's creative work may not be used without the owner's permission.

The "fair use" exemption to U.S. copyright law exists to allow things such as commentary, parody, news reporting, research and education about copyrighted works. This can be done without the permission of the author. Fair use is generally a short excerpt and almost always credited to the owner.

How does this affect blogging?

1. Comments made on your blog are taken as an implied license to be displayed and used on your blog.
2. Linking to another website on your blog does not infringe another blogger's or website owner's copyright.
3. It is OK to quote someone or include a short excerpt. It should not replicate the "heart" of the work.
4. Don't use photos, video or website content from others without permission. Even if you credit the original author, there would still be copyright infringement.

This article was not written by a lawyer and it does not intend to constitute legal advice.

Creative Commons License

A Creative Commons license allows authors / creators of writings, art and music to place conditions on the use of copyright works by others. The license amends your Copyright with the permission for others to use your work in certain ways. They can choose restrictions they wish to assign to their works, all of this free of charge. The intention is to avoid the problems created by current copyright laws.

Creative Commons is a nonprofit organization launched in 2001 by lawyers, intellectual property experts and web publishers. The Creative Commons website allows holders of copyright to clearly mark their work with icons that mark the work with Some Rights

Reserved or No Rights Reserved. Creative Works are set free for certain uses.

Creative Commons has a variety of licenses that allow copyright holders the ability to grant some or all rights to the public while retaining others through a variety of licensing and contract schemes. They supply digital documents in both plain English and legal wording. Digital codes are supplied to embed in websites according to the type of license.

Licenses are in 6 major types of licenses plus a public domain dedication. They vary between allowing commercial and non commercial sharing as well as rights to change and remix the work. Visit the Creative Commons website for more info at: creativecommons.org

Currently Google and Yahoo have Creative Commons search for content on the web which is reusable or modifiable. You can search for photos, music, text, books, educational material, and more. Yahoo now offers a Creative Commons Search API which can be worked into web applications.

Rules for Use of images

Images: Addition of photos and images makes your posts visually more appealing. The use of the images can be a little confusing. There are a number of Do's and Don'ts on the use of images in blogging and websites.

1. It is OK to display a "thumbnail" version of a photograph on a web site without permissions. This is considered "fair use" under US Copyright Laws and not an infringement.
2. It is NOT OK to link to an image hosted on another website without permission. This is sometimes called "inline linking"

3. It is OK to use pictures of people for editorial purposes (non-advertising) without their permission. People have a right to profit, and exclude someone else from profiting on their photograph or likeness.
4. It is NOT OK to modify a copyrighted image and then call it your own. Modifying a work, say by cropping, coloring, distorting, enlarging, etc. is not a way around Copyright laws.
5. It is OK to use someone's concept and create your own original image as long as no part of the original is directly copied. Merely using an original work as a model or inspiration does not by itself constitute an infringement.
6. It is NOT OK to copy images from foreign publications without getting permission. The US is part of the Berne Convention, and the Universal Copyright Convention. With these treaties, works produced in foreign countries enjoy the same copyright protections within the United States.
7. It is OK to use royalty free photos. You are then licensed to use these photos and images and do not need to pay a royalty each time a photo is viewed.

This article was not written by a lawyer and it does not intend to constitute legal advice.

Fired For Blogging

Blogging provides an easy way to publish information of all types to a worldwide audience. If that writing involves information considered sensitive by employers, employees are feeling the consequences.

It is less about being fired for blogging and more about disclosing sensitive information in a public forum that is getting employees into trouble. Bloggers write about their lives, discuss hobbies and talk about their work. But complaining about co-workers, disclosing confidential information or posting inappropriate pictures have gotten bloggers fired in recent years.

Heather Armstrong
In 2002, Heather Armstrong, a Web designer was fired for writing satirical accounts of her work including coworkers on her blog titled Dooce. This is the source of the term "Dooced" which means to be fired because of comments made by an employee on a personal blog.

Ellen Simonetti
Ellen Simonetti was a Delta Airlines flight attendant who was fired for "inappropriate pictures in uniform on the Web." Ellen apparently posted photographs of herself on her blog in her Delta Air Lines uniform aboard a company airplane. One photo apparently showed the 30-year-old with her Delta uniform blouse partially unbuttoned and was deemed suggestive.

Mark Jen
Mark Jen is a former Google employee who was fired for making comments on financial performance and future Google products on his blog. Apparently, he candidly criticized Google on a variety of subjects including their intranet, his work laptop and his compensation.

Michael Hanscom
In 2003 Michael Hanscom, a Microsoft contractor, lost his job after he took some pictures of Apple G5 computers being unloaded onto the software company's campus and posted them to his blog. Apparently Microsoft has a "no camera" rule on campus.

Blogging is a very public forum and divulging something about your employer can spell trouble at work.

It usually takes three weeks to prepare a good impromptu speech.
- Mark Twain

Chapter 8 Blog Writing

Writing blog posts and making comments on blogs is actually very simple. Your writing should be clear, concise, lively, factual, and optimized for the search engines. There are no hard and fast rules on blog writing, only guidelines to follow.

1. **Create a plan and follow it:** If your goal is business blog marketing, write your postings around a core subject. If you are promoting your plumbing company, write postings about plumbing issues.
2. **Keep it short and sweet:** Using short sentences are best. Aim at keeping your posts at about 250 words. Use bulleted points or a numbered list whenever you can. In blog writing, less is more. Keep sentences and paragraphs short.
3. **Make it fun to read:** Don't be afraid to write with personality. People like people they can relate to. Also remember that people trust people that they consider authorities.
4. **Linking is important:** Each post should have links to previous posts, quoted sources, definitions, articles, products, bios and more. Use links to support your opinions and statements.
5. **Link Text is Important:** If one of the purposes of your blog is to promote your business website, then use keywords in the link text to promote your business website to the search engines.
6. **Ask questions to engage your readers:** Asking questions is a good way to get comments back and to start a two way conversation. Watch your statistics and see what topics get the most attention.
7. **Encourage comments:** Make it easy for your readers to comment. Avoid registrations before comments can be made. Comments are the lifeblood of a business blog. Ask your readers for information, opinions and experiences.

Selecting Your Blog Topic

You have made the decision that business blog marketing is an important marketing strategy. Now, what should you be writing about?

Focus is very important in selecting your blog topic. One reason for blogging is to be considered an authority on your subject. A narrow, tightly focused definition can produce more traffic and better SEO results than a broad set of subjects. General, all purpose discussions confuse the search engines and won't do as well.

There are 4 steps in selecting your blog topic:

1. **What interests your customers?** It should be closely related to your business and catch prospects while they are making their buying decision. As an example, if you sell baby furniture, blog about choosing a baby name. People generally choose a name before they buy furniture.
2. **What are you passionate about?** Writing a blog takes dedication and commitment. It is much easier to write about something that interests you and that you are excited about.
3. **Narrow your niche.** Nowadays even a blog specifically about Home Decorating is too broad. A blog about Window Treatments would be more focused. You will more likely be seen as an expert in this narrowed topic area.
4. **Research keywords and traffic.** Use one of the keyword research tools available to make sure there is sufficient traffic. Select the phrases you should be using as you write.

If you want more traffic and you want to do better with the search engines, a very narrowly defined blogging topic is always better. You just want to make sure you have enough content to be able to keep the blog going.

Niche Blogging

Focused niche blogs get results much faster than blogs that deal with multiple topics. The Internet is filled with a massive amount of information. Focused writing allows a niche blog to stand out.

Search engines quickly recognize the subject of a niche blog and reward this focus with good search engine rankings.

A niche blog focuses on a market segment and possibly a niche demographic. A blog focused on fashion wouldn't be considered a niche blog, yet one focused on trendy junior fashions would be. In this case the demographic creates the niche.

To set-up a good niche blog, select a topic that is popular and one that you know about. Start your blog by writing one entry each day. Watch your blog's traffic statistics carefully. You will quickly see which postings generate the most interest. Modify your writing topics and writing style based on your audience response.

What makes a good niche blog?

1. **Keyword Research**: Use one of the keyword research tools to determine the level of interest and competition for your subject. Look for a large number of searches with only a limited competition.
2. **Tightly focused content:** All postings should be around a single subject area. This requires that the topic be approached from multiple angles or perspectives.
3. **Narrow subject**: Focus on a segment of the market and go into great depth with detail. Be an expert and dominate your chosen niche.

4. **Fresh Material**: A good niche is wide enough to allow for a large number of postings that allow fresh and new insight. There has to be long-term value for your readers.

Blogging Must Add Value

Should every business blog? The answer is a clear yes… as long as they have something to contribute of value. Good blog marketing is about delivering interesting and useful content to the blogosphere. Blogging without adding value is just adding noise to an already busy Internet. This noise actually hurts a company's marketing effort.

So what should a business blog about? First, you need to identify who you are trying to reach. This is your targeted audience. This could be customers, employees, shareholders or maybe a particular market segment.

Once you have identified your audience, then figure out what they are interested in reading about that is closely aligned with your product or service. As an example, if you are a Real Estate Appraiser, you may blog about housing value trends in your area as a resource to buyers and sellers. If you are a book printer, you may blog about how to go about publishing a book as an aid to would be authors.

Having a content plan is an important step in launching a blog. It insures that you will connect with your targeted audience and develop a readership that builds. Building a readership will also build your business.

Plan Before You Write

Spend time planning before writing. This makes for a better, more focused posting. For some, jotting down an outline with the key points is all that is required. The key is to write with the reader in mind and to deliver a posting with good value.

Blog Plan: From time to time, check back to your original planning document where you outlined the objectives of your blog. Look at your visitor traffic statistics, which postings are most read? Which postings receive the most comments? Are you achieving the results you wanted? If not, then take a good hard look at your blogging … or at your plan.

Stay focused: Try to avoid addressing a large variety of subjects in your business blog. Stay as targeted as possible. This way you will build a following of readers in your niche market.

Solve a problem: Readers are looking for solutions to a problem they have. Will your posting help them solve some issue or help do something better? As you write, remember your audience. Write about things that will help them, inform them, amuse them, inspire them, and encourage them.

Begin with the end: What do you want to accomplish? Write the ending and then you will find the rest of your story falls in place in a clear logical sequence.

Choose a catchy title: This is what get's your readers' attention in both the RSS feeds and the search engine results. This is a great place to include your keywords.

"If you don't know where you are going any road will take you there." -- Through the Looking Glass: Lewis Carroll

Targeting Your Blog Audience

Identifying and connecting with your readership is vital to the success of your blog. Who are your best prospects? Focusing on your target audience allows you to address their goals and interests. Writing about these subjects, from different angles and with captivating storylines will convert more followers.

Identifying Your Target

Who are you trying to reach? What niche market are you going after? Your blog audience tends to be different than your typical customer. Blog readers tend to be more knowledgeable, more technical and more up to date on the latest developments. They read multiple blogs to stay up to date. It is important to plan and write to attract only those readers.

What to write about?

What is it that your selected audience wants to read about? Choose a topic that your ideal prospect wants to read about.

If you were a seller of baby furniture and you want to reach first time parents, then you may want to write about naming a baby. This way you reach your targeted readers at about the same time they are buying baby furniture. Of course you would have links on your blog to your baby furniture website.

Conversational tone

Writing should be informal, honest and conversational. Blogs give your readers a glimpse of your personality. You should use terms, phrases and even colloquialisms that they will recognize. Your postings should build trust. Your objective is to connect with your readers so they will return and ultimately contact you when they need what you have to offer.

No matter how intriguing your subject, how well written the posting, if you fail to reach your audience, you have missed your target.

5 Ways of Differentiating Your Blog

There are many millions of blogs out there; many dealing with the same subject as yours. How do you get noticed with such competition? People make their choices based on differences. To make your blog a runaway success, you need to differentiate it from all the rest out there.

How do you get your blog to stand out from the crowd? Here are 5 ways to make your blog memorable.

1. **Personality:** Readers are attracted to blogs written with more personality. People respond well to strong personalities because they are more entertaining. Developing your own uniqueness and your own voice helps develop your following.
2. **Passion:** Passion is inspiring, captivating and draws people in. People listen when you speak strongly with conviction and confidence. After all, if you feel strongly then it must be true.
3. **Headlines:** A catchy headline will bring in a stream of new visitors. As people browse blog engines such as Technorati, they are scanning the headlines. Be different, be bold and be eye catching.
4. **Openers:** The first paragraph is the most important except for the headline. Grab their attention with the first few lines. This draws people in and if it is interesting, then they will continue reading. If it is dull, then you have lost them.
5. **Depth:** People read blogs for information. Don't brush over the subject but write with detail and with examples. Depth does not mean lengthy, it is important to be concise in your writing. Link to your resources, this allows your readers to explore if they wish.

Daring to be different is important to success. Seth Godin suggests "Do the never." Remember when toothpaste was only available in squeezable tubes and never any other way?

Habits of Highly Effective Bloggers

Effective blogging uses many of the concepts from one of my favorite books: The Seven Habits of Highly Effective People by Steven Covey. These following seven habits help bloggers to be better business blog marketers.

1. **Blog proactively**. By this I mean be a leader and an expert. This means thinking and acting ahead and not just reacting to situations. Let your personality out and be authentic and honest. Deliver content based on your principles and values.
2. **Blog with a plan in mind**. Know the purpose of your blog and who your targeted audience is. Create a content plan that focuses on your niche market. Choose subjects and topics that will be especially interesting to your targeted readers.
3. **Put your plan into action**. Write original interesting postings that focus on your targeted topics. Address the interests of your targeted audience. Use blog titles that catch the reader's attention. Most of all stay focused.
4. **Think win-win**. This is an important secret to personal and professional success. Encourage fellow bloggers; especially beginners give credit and links as often as possible. Give useful information to your readers and be liberal in giving helpful advice.
5. **Understand your readers**. Make your blog interesting and easy to use for your targeted readers. Use your traffic statistics and the comments you receive as feedback on which topics create the most interest.

Understand Their Readers

Plan and Put Plans into Action

Are an Expert in Their Field

Highly Effective Bloggers

Encourage Collaboration

Seek Self Improvement

Helpful to Other Bloggers

6. **Think collaboration.** Blogging is a social media and is meant to involve people. Actively participate in commenting by leaving insightful and appropriate comments. Encourage comments and respond in a way that establishes relationship with your readers.

7. **Improve yourself.** Blog regularly and set a regular time and place for blogging. Budget time as part of your schedule. Read other blogs regularly to generate ideas and

to interact with others. Investigate new ideas and expand your understanding for personal growth.

Research Tools for Blog Writing

There are a number of excellent tools that help in researching topics for blogging. For business blog marketing, these research tools allow you to bring current, interesting and pertinent information into your blog postings.

1. **Google Alerts**: This is a free email alert service. Just enter in the search term that you are researching and Google Alerts will send an email daily, weekly or as it happens. Google delivers snippets of web pages or news stories directly to your email box.

2. **Feed Reader**: Feeds are incredibly useful for research. Feed aggregators such as Bloglines; deliver new postings and information directly to your desktop. Simply subscribe to the RSS feed from a blog or website that you are interested in and you can receive new blog postings, podcasts, online news and even weather forecasts as they are updated.

3. **Google Trends**: View popularity of topics over time. Based on Google search data, graphs of search volume are available. Enter up to five topics and see how often they've been searched on Google over time. Graphs show the relative popularity of each search term over a specified period of time - up to two years.

4. **Keyword Research Tool**: Wordtracker and Keyword Discovery are the most popular paid tools. There are a number of good ones that are free. Google has a good one that shows relative search and Adwords competition data.

5. **SEODigger**: This is a powerful analyzer. Discover which

keywords any website is being ranked for on Google. This is limited to websites with positions in the top 20 results.

6. **Delicious.com**: This is a social bookmarking site where the bookmarks are completely searchable by keyword tags. These are all high quality resources that others have thought enough of to bookmark.

Nielsen NetRatings

Nielsen NetRatings is a great source for Internet trend and usage statistics. They are an Internet media and market research firm that conduct studies for private firms that want to understand consumer attitudes and behavior. They publish regular public reports on subjects such as search engine trends. They provide BlogPulse which is a blog search engine along with research tools.

Many of us grew up hearing about the Nielsen ratings for television shows. Nielsen NetRatings is a branch of the same organization. Nielsen has been around for over 50 years and provides marketing research statistics for nearly all types of media.

So why is Nielsen NetRatings important to business blog marketing? They supply publicly available information that helps understand our customer's behavior and how they spend their time online. By going to their website (www.nielsen-netratings.com) we can find out all sorts of interesting bits of information.

Did you know that the average Internet user (October 2007) spends 55 minutes in a surfing session and will spend an average of 46 seconds on each web page? For September 2007, Google was the top brand with a total unique audience of 112 million people. Nextag was the top advertiser for the same time period by delivering 24.4 billion ads.

Nielsen also publishes the BlogPulse website which tracks blog trends and statistics. BlogPulse is a blog search engine and it contains tools such as:

1. **Trend Search:** Create your own graphs about specific search terms.
2. **Featured Trends:** Identifies the topics and subjects being discussed in blogs.
3. **Conversation Tracker:** Creates a threaded view of conversations based on posts.

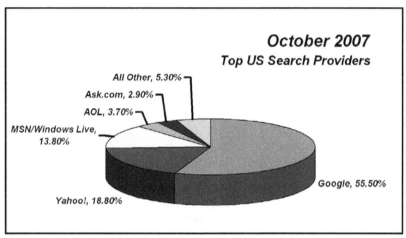

Source: Nielsen Online December 2007

What is FeedBurner?

FeedBurner is a true web 2.0 service that makes it easy for any visitor to subscribe to a blog feed regardless of which feed reader or news reader they prefer to use. It is a service that takes normal RSS or Atom feeds and turns (burns) them into a feed that can then be distributed to readers for use in any RSS reader. It simplifies the RSS Feed.

142

Sometimes called a feed enhancer, FeedBurner takes your feed and adds more functionality to it without you having to modify it yourself. FeedBurner also allows your readers to subscribe via email. Published feeds are modified in several ways, including automatic links to Digg and del.icio.us, and "splicing" information from multiple feeds.

You will also be able to easily activate "Feed Flares" which are third party developer programs that add more functionality to your feed. Popular "Feed Flares" include:

1. Google Bookmark This
2. Bookmark With Yahoo! Bookmarks
3. Submit item to Kontrib
4. Rate Me On Authorati
5. Track with co.mments
6. My Digg Counts
7. Alexa Rank
8. Blog This
9. Add to Technorati Favorites
10. Find Related Feeds

FeedBurner was acquired by Google in June 2007. Google continues to expand into the Web 2.0 world of blogging with companies like Blogger, FeedBurner and Measure Map (blog visitor statistics). Measure Map technology has been integrated into Google Analytics.

We routinely add FeedBurner to each blog site we produce because it definitely drives more repeat visitors back to your blog.

Great Blog Titles Attract Readers

75% of Ads in the Sunday newspaper are skipped because they don't grab the reader's attention. A powerfully titled blog article will draw visitors in from their feed readers. Your headline must capture attention. Your headline should make it seem as though getting the information in your article is vital to the reader's very existence.

There are two goals in writing an effective title. First is to catch the reader's attention and draw them in. Second is to get listed on the search engines so searchers will find you.

Your keyword or phrase MUST be in your title! This is what you want the search engines to notice. As you write your blog, try to write titles that match what you would search for if you were looking on a search engine.

What kinds of titles work? Try these to get attention.

1. **Please Skip This [subject].** No, no. I told you to skip this and… Curiosity is overpowering and most people can't resist.
2. **Little Known Ways to [how to].** An intriguing way of getting the reader's attention similar to "The Secret of…" headline.
3. **Myth [believable].** People love myths… or there wouldn't be a show called Mythbusters.
4. **Here's a Quick Way to [solve a problem].** People love quick and easy solutions.
5. **5 Things that will ruin …** This uses two things that grab attention. Fear and people love to read lists.

Make titles that are descriptive, clever, and clear. You are writing titles for two audiences: readers and search engines. Choose your words carefully and focus on action if possible.

Format of a Blog Posting

Writing a blog posting is different than writing an article or a book. Blog readers have short attention spans; they need to be able to scan thru your content quickly and easily. Blog postings are short, easily scanned and quick to read.

1. **Can be scanned:** Your reader should be able to quickly glance through your posting and pick up the main points. Use lists, images, tables, sub-headlines, examples, indented notes, indented quotes, icons, colors, bold and italics to break up your article and make it easier to scan.
2. **Short posting:** A typical blog posting should be about 250 words and be written in a simple format. The longer a post goes, the more people skim, and the less likely they are to get the information they really want.
3. **Short paragraphs:** Blog writing is best using shorter sentences and paragraphs for easier reading. Readers want information fast and in small digestible chunks. Use paragraphs of about 50 to 100 words or roughly 3 sentences long and break them up with bold subheadings.
4. **Keep it simple:** Simple means getting rid of extra words. Simple writing is persuasive. A writer's ability to edit himself is probably the most important blog writing technique.
5. **Use Easy to read fonts:** Unusual font choices and other poor formatting choices can make something visually difficult to read.

"A good argument in five sentences will sway more people than a brilliant argument in a hundred sentences." – Writing Tip from Scott Adams (Creator of Dilbert)

Writing Blogs with Style

Blog readers are a different breed. They expect a certain easy to read style. They expect writing to have personality. Nothing turns off a blog reader faster than a condescending or harsh writing style.

1. **Topic**: Are you suffering from writer's block? Maybe you are just not passionate about the subject you are writing about. Write about something you know well, something specific. Avoid general and wide sweeping subjects.

2. **Audience**: If you don't have a clear understanding of your audience, you won't know what messages will excite them. What does the reader want to know? In writing, use terms and phrases they will recognize and identify with.

3. **Original Content**: New and original content will get your reader's attention. Simply quoting others and echoing other people's content is boring. Blogging is about experimenting and discovering what works for you and your audience.

4. **Action Words**: These are verbs like "make", "do", "write", "take", and "build." When people are searching, they like to be told "what to do." Tell them.

5. **Spelling and Grammar**: Mistakes distract people from the content they are reading. Even though blogs may be less formal.

6. **Be Entertaining**: Come up with an entertaining angle and use interesting language to be a hit with your readers.

7. **Call to Action**: A clear call to action at the end of a posting will increase the likelihood readers will act.

"The secrets of telling a story well are three: 1. How to end. 2. Where to begin. 3. What to leave out." – Roy H. Williams

Blog Postings: How Much and How Often?

How long should a blog posting be? How often should you post? Our stock answer is a typical posting should be 250 words and postings should be no less than 3 times per week. Here is why.

Reader Attention Span: The typical web reader has a short attention span. Studies show that the average blog reader will stay on a blog up to 96 seconds. To be effective, content needs to be presented in easily read chunks. This puts the maximum at about 500 words.

SEO: Both extremely short and extremely long pages are not well ranked with the search engines. For blogs, the optimal length seems to be around 250 words. Postings under 150 words do not seem to rank as well on the search engines.

Posting Frequency: It's not enough to just post frequently, you actually have to say something important. Keeping the quality content flowing is the best way to bring in traffic. Readers seem to prefer 3-7 postings per week.

The top two reasons that people will unsubscribe to a blog are:
1. Too many blog postings and the post levels will overwhelm.
2. Infrequent posting and the blog is effectively dead.

Myth: More postings will give your blog a higher Google PageRank. This is wrong. Google's new Blog PageRank algorithm rewards consistent posting rates more than how many total postings.

Posting length can and should vary by how much you have to say. They should range from 150 to 500 words. Posting frequency should be 3-7 times per week.

Making Comments to Blogs

The ability to make comments and respond to postings is what makes a blog a blog. For both personal and business blogging, comments are the feedback that adds spice to these online conversations. Blog writers will post information they think is important, but it is the comments that reinforce what is important to readers. Comments are what change a monologue into collaboration.

The vast majority of readers leave a blog without leaving a comment or contributing to it in any way. The best kinds of comments do come from thoughtful people who add more information about a topic. Good blog commenting adds to the discussion and builds the commenter's reputation for being knowledgeable, informative, friendly and engaged.

Guidelines for adding comments to blogs really are just proper blogging etiquette. What are some good guidelines?

1. Don't change the subject.
2. Keep comments short and to the point.
3. Contribute and add to the conversation.
4. Read the entire posting plus comments before adding your comments.
5. Don't spam by trying to sell your product or service.
6. Refrain from personal attacks or being disrespectful of others.

Blog Comment Guidelines

As you begin blogging, you will receive comments from your readers. After all, many times the most interesting content comes from the comments. Some comments will be relevant and helpful while others will be plain junk. Establishing guidelines will help keep your blog free of comment spam and inappropriate language.

Setting up guidelines on how you will respond and what types of comments are acceptable will make decisions easier. Here is an example of a comment policy that you are free to use or modify:

Comment Policy
We welcome your comments to our blog. To keep our blog focused and to protect you and other users of the site, we have set some comment guidelines.

1. This Blog is moderated and comments submitted will be reviewed before being posted. We reserve the right to edit or delete comments.
2. Comment spam will be immediately deleted. This includes comments that are focused on selling a product or service or are not relevant to the posting. We do not allow marketing messages of any kind.
3. Please keep your comments brief and on topic. Comments longer than 1-2 paragraphs make the blog difficult to use. We reserve the right to edit to make comments concise and clear. We will exclude comments not related to the subject.
4. Relevant links that point to your own or someone else's site that is relevant to the topic is encouraged. Comments with a link in it that has no relevance to the blog posting will be deleted.
5. Please refrain from personal attacks or being disrespectful of others. Do not use profanities or other offensive or objectionable words. Comments may be deleted or edited that include such language.
6. Please post only your own work and do not post words or materials that were taken from somewhere else. Do not infringe on the copyright rights of others.

7. Please respect people's privacy. Do not share anyone's address, place of employment, telephone number or email address.
8. Comments that appear to violate laws that govern use of copyrights, trade secrets, etc., will be deleted. We reserve the right not to publish allegations, conspiracy theories and other information which we know to be false or unsubstantiated.
9. If you are under 18, please get a parent's or guardian's permission before posting any comments.

Comment guidelines make blogging, moderating comments and responding easier on yourself and your readers. There are no surprises and all parties know what to expect. The tone and wording of a comment policy should match your blog.

Product Reviews

Product reviews are excellent blogging material and help consumers and businesses find out if a product is worthwhile. Product reviews can either be an individual product or comparisons of products.

As a reviewer, you are writing for the benefit of the reader. Someone will be using your opinion to decide if they should be buying this product. It is your job to provide useful advice. The product review centers around 4 basic questions:

1. **Who is the reader?** The review will be written differently for a technical user than for a retail consumer. What solution are they looking for?
2. **What does the product promise?** You need to understand everything about the product. Read all available literature, documentation and instructions completely.

3. **How well does it work?** Does it solve the problem? Did it do the job as advertised? Were the features useful?
4. **Recommendation:** Does this product offer good value and would you buy it?

Review Format
The format of the review is pretty straight forward.

1. **Introduction:** States the problem to be solved, and introduces the product as a possible solution. In a single sentence state whether you liked it or were disappointed.
2. **Body:** Describe what the product does, and how it works. The purpose is to describe what it promises. Then, go into detail about what you like, and what you dislike.
3. **Conclusion:** Give a strong recommendation for purchase (or not) based on your conclusions. Is it worth the money? …and explain why.
4. **Photos:** Include a product photo in all reviews.

"It is not the employer who pays wages -- he only handles the money. It is the product who pays the wages." -- Henry Ford

Blog Press Release

A good press release starts with something worth announcing. Uninteresting news gets little results. Our sample is just a guide for the structure of a press release.

FOR IMMEDIATE RELEASE:

ABC Inc. Announces Cure for the Common Cold

Create an active and descriptive headline to capture the reader's attention. It needs to be written for both search engines and consumers.

SUMMARY: Write a brief summary of the press release that helps clarify the headline, and describes what the press release is about.

Body: Answer the Where, When, Who, and What. Write using the inverted pyramid format, placing less important information further down. The press release should be approximately 500 words. Keep your sentences and paragraphs short; a paragraph should be no more than 3-4 sentences.

First Paragraph: Include City, State - Month Day, Year - Organization Name - Answer the "what" in the rest of this paragraph.

Second paragraph of the body should connect the first paragraph to more detailed information about the "why" and the "how" of the news event.

Additional paragraphs should contain supporting information, industry statistics, and quotes.

Last paragraph should include your call to action. This is your opportunity to prompt your target audience to do something. ### (Use three number signs to denote where the press release ends)

CORPORATE SUMMARY: Short summary about your organization.

CONTACT INFORMATION: Include the contact information of a person the media can follow up with. (Name, Company Name, Phone Number, E-mail Address, Company URL)

After posting to your blog, email the media representatives that you want to especially reach with a link to your blog posting.

The Case Study

Stories are a powerful way to illustrate a lesson. Real life stories are even more powerful and interesting. Case studies present your products or services and show what they can do. They are interesting blogging materials to build up visitor traffic.

A case study is a description of a real situation with complex issues. They fit classroom theories into real life. The challenge in blog writing is to write what is typically a long story into a 250 word posting. You want to grab their attention from the start... and then keep it!

Think of the case study as a three act play:
1. Problem
2. What you did
3. Benefits and Results

Problem: This is where you introduce the problem. Stick to one problem and explain how you can solve it in measurable terms. Present important background issues. Write about something that has significant business pain for the reader. The problem should be specific that your readers will relate to.

What You Did: This is where you introduce your product or service and how it will solve the problem. Tell the story and allow the events to unfold. Readers are looking for something to be revealed. Allow readers to "see" the pain point and the evolving events in their imagination.

Benefits and Results: A good case study keeps the readers in suspense. They are caught up in the events, the pain and what could be. This is where readers find out if the solution worked, what the consequences were and what changes happened.

8 ways to Keep Your Blog Subscribers

Darren Rowse did an interesting study on "34 Reasons Why
Readers Unsubscribe from Your Blog." We went in and analyzed
his data to come up with our own "8 ways to keep your blog
subscribers."

1. **Keep it interesting**: People are searching for new and
   original information. The number one reason that people
   unsubscribe is that they find the content uninteresting, low
   quality or that the blog is using recycled content.
2. **Don't post too often**: Too much content overwhelms your
   readers. It really depends on how long each posting is, but
   posting over 3 times per day is generally considered too
   often.
3. **Keep focused**: People subscribe because they want to learn
   more about a particular topic. If you change the topic or
   keep changing subjects, you will lose your readership.
4. **Post regularly**: Even a few posts each month will hold
   onto subscribers. Too few of posts and the blog will
   become stale or "dead."
5. **Post full feeds**. Resist using partial feeds. Partial feeds are
   when only a snippet of the post is published and you have
   to click through to the blog to read the entire thing.
6. **Resist selling**: The focus of the blog should be on
   presenting information, commentaries and opinions. Avoid
   direct selling and self promotion. Nothing turns readers off
   faster than a sales pitch.
7. **Write clearly**: Make it easy on your readers so they can
   clearly understand you. Poor writing style, bad grammar or
   a difficult to read format makes your readers work too hard.
8. **Stay positive**: Opinions and commentaries are great, they
   are entertaining and interesting. What turns people off is
   negative and offensive language... or just being too pushy.

Increasing Return Traffic to Your Blog

Having regular traffic and visitors is important to a business blog and to business blog marketing. It is even more important to develop a loyal readership and return traffic. Does your blog offer content that would give visitors a reason to return? If not, you need to get to work.

1. **Content is king:** The three most important ways to develop your readership is to post interesting material, post regularly and to post often. Regular postings also brings back the search engine spiders frequently to index your site.
2. **Write to your audience:** Target readers who are likely to become customers and write about topics that they want to read about. Focus on developing an interested readership that is the same as your customer base.
3. **Write with style:** Keep it fresh and mix it with a little humor. Opinions and commentaries are great, they are entertaining and interesting. You need to take every opportunity to provide a good blog reader experience.
4. **Easy to subscribe:** Make it easy for visitors to subscribe to your RSS feed. Add prominent RSS subscription icons or button in a prominent location. If someone reads something they like, encourage them to subscribe.
5. **Organization:** Categorize your topics into logical topics and include a search box. Make it easy to find postings on subjects that interest them. Good organization entices people to read multiple postings.
6. **Watch traffic statistics:** Watch which topics and postings get the best response. This will give you quick feedback on what your readers are hungry for. Writing regularly about subjects your readers are looking for, will quickly grow your loyal reader base.

Unfocused Blogging Fails to get Results

Is your blog writing focused or unfocused? Should you have a purpose for your blogging? If you want good results, your blog should reflect your goals.

Business blog marketing is very different than personal blogging. Personal blogs in many instances are a form of an online diary. Business blogs on the other hand should be focused toward a purpose. This could be branding, building a readership, etc.

What happens when a blog is unfocused?
1. **Readers are confused**: Mixing subjects is hard on your audience. A blog that is about commercial real estate should not give advice on relationships. Readers are less likely to return to a blog that discusses a variety of topics.
2. **Damages your image**: Rambling shows lack of focus and disorganization. Readers interpret this as someone that can't stay on task. If branding yourself as an expert is important, then a focused blog is important.
3. **Lower Search Rankings**: Aimlessly wandering postings confuse the search engines and they are not able to identify the topic of your blog. An unfocused blog is unlikely to appear on the important first page of search engine results.

Blogs that are focused on a central topic will:
1. Build up a loyal readership much more quickly.
2. Bring in targeted visitors.
3. Get regular returning visitors.
4. Connect with your audience.
5. Separates your blog from others in your field.
6. Create a more professional image.
7. Cause you to think more deeply and write better.
8. Develop respect for you as an expert by your readers.
9. Generate higher quality sales leads.
10. Get better search engine rankings.

Using Website Statistics to Build Blog Traffic

Traffic statistics is one of the best measurement systems available to the blogger. This gives almost immediate feedback to how each posting is being received by your readers. Almost any of the traffic statistics packages out there will give you the basic information you need to build your readership.

Traffic statistics measure effectiveness of blog titles, content you are writing and the comments you are making on other blogs. Don't obsess over your site statistics but use them as a tool to find out what your visitors find interesting.

1. **Overall Trend** – Is there a steady increase in traffic coming to your blog? I watch the total number of visits, the number of unique visitors and the volume of visits each day. If you take your monthly totals and divide the total visits by the unique visitors, you will get the number of times the average visitor came back to your blog.
2. **Most Popular** – Which postings are attracting the most traffic? I will look at the daily traffic and see which days had a spike in traffic. I then look at which articles appeared that day and try and figure out what I did that brought in more readers.
3. **Referral Traffic** – Which sites are sending you visitors? Visit the site and investigate if it is a link from a website, a blog posting or perhaps a link in a comment that you have left.
4. **Referring Search Engines** – Which search engines are referring visitors to you? You are probably ranked well for one or more search terms on this engine.
5. **Keywords** – Which keyword phrases are you being found for? Find the posting that is generating the traffic and see what you did. If this is a phrase you are targeting, see how you can do this again.

6. **Bounce Rate** – Some Statistics packages such as Google Analytics show Bounce Rate. This is the percentage of people who leave your website without viewing any extra pages. Bounce rates under 50% are good, if it is greater than 75% then you need to make some changes.

Nothing beats writing good interesting content. Traffic statistics are an excellent way to find out what strikes your reader's fancy.

Breaking Thru Blog Writer's Block!

Every blog writer who posts regularly will go through dry spells where they struggle to come up with meaningful topics to write about. The first thing to remember is that blogs are not novels so don't worry about creating that perfect posting.

Here are some ideas to help break thru writer's block and get those ideas flowing.

1. **Plan ahead**: Look at your blog plan. What topics did you plan on writing about? Should you expand your plan? I keep a list of writing subjects and jot down new ideas when they hit me.
2. **Read, read, and read**: Spend time each day reading other blogs related to your topic. Bookmark those that you find very interesting. Go back thru your bookmarked articles when you need new ideas.
3. **Search Engines**: Go to your favorite search engine and start typing in pertinent random phrases. See what topics grab your interest until you find that right topic.
4. **Choose your time**: Write when you are at your best. For me it is early in the morning and before my day starts. If this still isn't working, vary your time and try writing off hours when you're beyond tired.
5. **Clear your mind**: Try closing your eyes and meditating for a few minutes. Go do some chores such as mowing the

grass or washing dishes. It's amazing how ideas can come when you take a break.

6. **Easy Stuff**: If you have several writing projects, choose the one that is the easiest and most interesting to get started with.

Blogging takes dedication and commitment. It's important to keep blogging even when you are temporarily stumped about what to write next. Pretty soon you will have a flood of new ideas and you can't write fast enough.

Using Your Blog to Generate Leads

What are some good ways to generate leads? You can become an expert in your industry. You can reach out and communicate regularly with prospects to build a relationship. That is what blogging does. Add a good call to action and you have an effective lead generating tool.

Expert reputation: How can you communicate to the world that you are an expert? By making yourself visible in a public forum, you will be thought of as an expert. Here are some examples.

1. Take up public speaking.
2. Become active in a trade or technical association.
3. Write white papers or books.
4. Write your own blog.

By blogging regularly, being specific, credible and knowledgeable, you build an expert reputation. You build a positive image that will encourage prospects to gravitate toward you.

Communicate regularly: By blogging a brief, concise message that communicates well, you build up a readership that comes back over and over. Blogging allows you to regularly converse with people interested in what you have to say.

Build a relationship: Your blog becomes the virtual face for your business. Writing compelling posts draws your readers to you. The best way to convert a visitor into a loyal reader is to have the answers that they are seeking.

Call to action: Blogging is not about selling, it is about presenting interesting and engaging material. Having a clear link to a quote request form or other call to action can turn an interested reader into an interested prospect.

The ultimate purpose of a blog is to brand, to communicate and to build relationships. This is exactly what you need for lead generation.

Power of the Blogging Mindset

There is real power in the blogging mindset. In business blogging you become very focused on the wants, needs, issues, and interests of your targeted audience. The idea is to grow your readership by writing insightful and interesting content.

As you write blogs, your perspective and your way of thinking shift toward thinking about markets and customers. This shift into the blogging mindset is extremely beneficial for your business.

Blogging is like being an investigative reporter. If you are blogging successfully, part of your mind is always thinking about that next blog post. As you go thru each day, you become more observant and more focused. This makes you more effective in everything you do.

The blogging mindset:
1. **Alertness**: You become more alert and vigilant to what is going on around you. You are always on the prowl for new material.
2. **Questioning**: You analyze and question everything that goes on in your targeted market. You think in terms of cause and effect and look for the root cause.

3. **Researching**: As you find new things, you spend time investigating to understand your premise more fully. You explore new areas that you may not have considered before.
4. **Customer focused**: You look at things thru your customers eyes. After all, you want to build up your readership.
5. **Expert**: By thinking deeply, analyzing and watching your targeted niche, you keep expanding your knowledge and understanding. If you weren't an expert when you started, you become one.

The process of blogging creates the blogging mindset. The blogging mindset, if you are diligent, will make you a customer focused expert.

What is the distance between someone who achieves their goals consistently and those who spend their lives and careers merely following? -- The extra mile. --Gary Ryan Blair

Chapter 9 Blog Writing for SEO

While the main goal of your blog may be to express your thoughts, it is a powerful SEO tool that can promote your company website onto the search engines. Blogs actually have a great advantage over standard websites because of the great amount of new and fresh content that is posted.

In Blog writing, it is most important to use your targeted keyword phrases in your blog title and in the link text that links to your company website. Linking deep into your main website is more powerful and natural than just linking to a home page. Here are more SEO blog writing ideas.

1. **Keywords**: This is the foundation SEO strategy. These keywords should be used in titles, links, category names and even in the domain name.

2. **One topic per post**: The more tightly focused the theme of a page, the better when Search Engines come to rank it.

3. **Quality Content**: The best way to get links to your blog is to write quality content that people will want to read.

4. **Title**: Write keyword rich posting titles. The Title entices readers in and Titles are considered very important by the search engines.

5. **Keyword Rich Content**: Use keywords 1-2 times in the first few paragraphs. Search engines place more value on phrases in the first part of a posting.

6. **Keyword Linking**: Use key words in your posting and then link to the page in your company website that most closely fits that phrase.

7. **Products and Services**: Discuss specific products and services that you offer and then link directly to these pages making it easy for readers to learn more.

8. **Interlink your Sites**: This is the way Search Engines index your blog. We recommend that you provide some sort of site map or recommended sites list.

9. **Update regularly:** The more often that you update your blog the more often Search Engines will send their crawlers to your site to index it. We recommend that you blog no less than 3 times per week.

10. **Write optimal length posts**: There is some thought going around the Search Engine Optimization community that pages that are too short can get passed over for high rankings. Try to keep posts at about 250 words.

Blogging as a Traffic Building Strategy

Business blogs are a powerful search engine optimization tool. They bring benefits at many levels as part of a business marketing program. We use blog marketing in conjunction with normal SEO and we are getting powerful results.

Business blogging opens new markets to a business. It establishes that business as an authority and is a strong branding tool. Blogging is an interactive medium that allows a business to reach out to new customers.

We use blogging as part of our SEO campaigns. The heart of this is that it requires a business be willing to commit to regular blog postings of at least 3 times per week. Other key elements include a blogging plan with the correct keyword phrases being selected, the writing of interesting and original content and following our writing guidelines.

We knew we were getting superior SEO results by using SEO combined with blogging than with SEO alone. We went in and analyzed the results and were amazed at how much better the results were.

We went in and looked at results for stand-alone blogs (on a separate website than the main business website), the main business website and websites using our standard SEO process. We measured the number of unique visitors as our key indicator. Our sample was small. We used 3 blog sites, 3 business websites supported by blogs and 6 websites using standard SEO. The time period was 3 months.

Standard SEO showed a 39% increase in unique visitors. Blogs showed an 85% increase in unique visitors. Websites that were the primary recipient of links from the blog showed a whopping 123% increase in unique visitors.

I haven't been able to find any other similar analysis posted around the Internet and would be very interested to see what others are seeing using blogging for SEO.

Business Blogging as an SEO Strategy

Blog marketing is a two level strategy. First, business blogging allows you to reach a group of interested readers that your website and other traditional marketing strategies won't. Second and the subject of this posting, blogging generates a tremendous number of back links to both your blog website and to your main company website.

Blogging is an excellent linking strategy by attracting new theme related incoming links. Adding fresh content on a daily or every other day basis is rewarded by search engines with more frequent spidering and updating of search results.

Bloggers as a group are generous linkers that readily link back to source materials and provide an abundant number of natural and highly themed links. Bloggers will also create permanent links to their regularly read blogs from the home page of their blog.

A typical blog writer posts a daily or every other day entry to their business blog. Other bloggers who read these posts and find them interesting and relevant will link to the unique link of the blog posting called a permalink. This provides a valued one way link to the blog in what is called "deep linking." Deep linking helps the entire blog website be elevated in importance.

For blog marketing to be effective, the content must be fresh and interesting enough to attract readers and be good enough to get other bloggers to link to the postings. This is why blog postings are so highly valued by the search engines.

Using your blog and having a keyword plan and linking strategy is a great way to build the importance and website traffic to the company website. Not only do you get visitors clicking on the links in the blog which is broadcast via RSS, but the website rankings of the target website actually rises rather quickly.

Blogs are one of the hottest marketing delivery methods spreading through the business world today. Blogs are great tools to keep audiences informed and to help garner increased exposure. It is a great business development tool to increase your company visibility. Showcase your insights and knowledge to help get you recognized as an authority in your field.

Blogging is simply posting a journal of your commentaries and suggestions on whatever topics that your targeted customers are interested in. The technology for creating your own blog and then publishing out to the web is inexpensive and gives powerful results.

Practical SEO Tips for Blogs

Optimizing your blog for search engines is similar to SEO for websites but with some important differences. The goal is to bring more traffic to your blog. To do this, we need to increase search rankings on the regular Internet search engines such as Google as well as the blog search engines.

Selecting the correct keywords is the foundation for all search engine optimization for websites and blogs. These are the phrases that people will type in to do searches. There are a number of good keyword research tools, some free and some you will need to pay a subscription fee.

Keywords: The first step for blog SEO includes choosing up to 5-6 good descriptive keywords for your blog. This will serve as a guide for the topics your blog will be covering. Use these keywords in the categories or labels in your blog.

Title: The title for each blog posting is what attracts readers and is very important to the search engines. Try to create an intriguing title that will catch a reader's attention and include one of your keyword phrases.

Linking: Getting links from other blogs builds the importance of your blog in the eyes of the search engines. There are a few ways to get these valuable links.
1. Use your Blogroll feature to trade links with related blogs that you respect.
2. Write postings with interesting and original content that others will naturally link to.

3. Provide some sort of tool or analysis that others will link to.
4. Create some sort of controversy that will kick off a "buzz" among other bloggers.

Readership: Nothing is more important than creating great content that will develop a targeted readership. Make it interesting to your targeted customer and those in your industry. Participate in blog discussions with other bloggers to bring them to your blog regularly.

Blogging as a Link Popularity Strategy

Having a business blog can play a powerful role for most traditional website businesses. Blog marketing is part of the cutting edge of Internet marketing and search engine optimization strategies. Business blogging is important for marketing, public relations, and adding fresh new content. This steady supply of content is one reason they get rated so highly in the major search engines.

Having a blog added to the company website or as a stand-alone blog website is a very effective way to increase link popularity. We have found that adding postings at least 3 times per week will boost link popularity. This is as long as the content posted is fresh, informative and interesting.

The core to this link popularity strategy includes placing links in the posting using your targeted keyword phrases (anchor text) and linking directly to the page in your website that discusses this topic (deep linking). This is most effective when the blog website is a separate website hosted on a separate server. The links should be as close to the start of the beginning of the posting as possible to be viewed by the search engines as more important.

The interesting result is a very fast boost in link popularity and an increase in website rankings. For this to work, it takes dedication in regular postings of interesting information written in a conversational writing style. It is this great content that causes these blog postings to be picked up and distributed to other websites via RSS. It is the embedded links that boost link popularity.

Blogs Need Link Love!

Link love is linking to blogs that you enjoy and admire. These links of "love" make these blogs more important in the eyes of the search engines. These links are important for pushing blogs up in the search engine rankings. Search engines see blogs receiving many links as more important and reward them with higher search rankings.

Link love leads to link popularity for blogs. These links not only improve the search positions, they bring a steady stream of visitor referral. The 80-20 rule says that 80% of your referral traffic will come from 20% of your links.

Search engines love links. In fact, they will only respect you if many others already link to you. Little links are good because they potentially develop into major refers over time.

Remember deep linking is natural in blogs. These are links to individual postings. They funnel link popularity to the home page as well as all other pages of your blog. This gives the entire blog the ability to rank well on hundreds of medium and long keyword phrases.

Here are 5 ways to build link popularity in blogs:

1. The basis for ranking well with a blog is to have original and interesting content that people want to read and link to.
2. Try word-of-mouth marketing or viral marketing. This is where you post a funny video or something so interesting or valuable that people instantly link to it.
3. Link Baiting: This is similar to viral marketing. There are a number of approaches that are used to get people to link back to your blog. This can include providing website or analysis tools or running some sort of competition or awards. Another approach is to take a controversial position or attack a prominent blogger hoping to attract links from other bloggers.
4. Trade links with other bloggers that you respect on your Blogroll.
5. Get links from directories where you can list your blog. Some are free such as DMOZ.org. Some are paid such as Dir.Yahoo.com or JoeAnt.com.

Choosing Keywords

All of your other Blog SEO strategies won't help you at all if you choose the wrong keywords. This is because all these strategies are built on top of the keywords. Keywords are how search engines index and classify your website.

So how do you pick the right keywords? You have to think like your customer. People search for solutions to what they need. They look for the product or service that satisfies their need. They do this more often than looking for the person who supplies the service.

Are you targeting researchers or buyers with your keyword phrases? Researchers are at the beginning of the selling cycle and they generally search for 1-2 word general phrases. Buyers search for much more specific 3-4 word phrases.

Use the language that your customers would use. A frequent mistake is to use language from the industry you are in. People who sell booths for exhibitions refer to them as "pop up displays". Yet their customers will search for "trade show displays" four times more often.

Competitors are a great source of intelligence. Go to your competitors and look at what terms or keyword phrases they are using. Read through their page text. What specific search terms are being used?

Once you choose your keywords, place them strategically and prominently on your web pages. Make sure they are used in a natural way and make good marketing sense. The language you use needs to be action oriented to convince your visitors to buy.

Domain Names are Important

Your domain name identifies your blog and is the way people will remember you. A domain name establishes your unique identity and creates an impression on visitors.

Using keywords to attract the search engines attention in the domain name is an important SEO strategy. Using your primary keyword phrase as your domain name will give you an edge over your competition. If your phrase is a very popular term, try using the term blog following the keyword or add a word such as "best" or "the" in front of your keyword phrase.

Another strong domain name is to use your product name. People instantly understand what you do and you create recognition. This can be good when you use this as part of your brand recognition strategy.

Keep the name as short a possible so it is easier to type and remember. Domain names can be as short as 2 characters or as long as 63. This does not include the extension such as .com. Examples range from American Airlines (aa.com) to didyouknowthatyoucanonlyhavesixty-threecharactersinadomain-name.com.

The ending for the domain name is the Top Level Domain (TLD). This is sometimes called the extension. 72% of the domains registered today are .COM's and 11% are .NET's. Staying with a COM or NET infers that your blog is established and has been around for some time.

Choosing a domain name is an important choice and is part of your Internet marketing strategy. This reflects strongly on the image of your business.

SEO for Video Blogging

Today search engines such as Google offer video searches. Google has introduced "Universal Search" that blends results from its websites, news, video, images and local search engines. The top video search engines are: Yahoo Video, YouTube.com, AOL Video, Google Video and Singingfish.com (owned by AOL).

Optimizing videos and images to use means adjusting the size and the speed of your content to make it efficient for downloading. Following are a few rules to help ensure that videos you include in your blog postings are found and indexed by the search engines.

Name your video using keywords separated by dashes. For example: preparing-house-for-sale.mov rather than 584219km.mov.

Use keywords in the META data. Always add a keyword-rich title tag and description to your video.
When linking to videos, use keywords in anchor text (link text). Surround your video with keyword rich content. Consider adding a transcript of your video.

Place your videos on pages named with the same keywords. This is done by including the keywords in the blog posting title.
The first and last frame should have keywords on the screen. Video search engines such as Blinkx and OCR will read them. Create a separate video sitemap. These sitemaps can be submitted to both video and content search engines.

Watch which video posts do the best and then replicate what you did.

Tip: *Watermark your video so when it is picked up by others and displayed around the Internet, your website and brand is carried with it.*

Should Your Blog and Website Be Separate?

That's a great question. It really depends on your business blog marketing goals. If SEO is a primary objective, then yes separate them. If branding is what you are after, then keep them together.

Reasons to keep them together:
1. The blog reinforces your main brand and you want to keep

the information together.
2. Adds website content and value in the eyes of search engines.
3. The focus of the blog closely matches the main website.
4. The blog supports an area of the main website such as the FAQ area.
5. Blog is designed to be part of and to support current marketing efforts.

Reasons to separate:
1. With separate domain the incoming links from the blog to your main website are more powerful because links come from an external source.
2. Domain name can be selected for maximum keyword effect.
3. The topics are different and your blog will be more accepted by readers and be more "linkable" by other blogs.
4. The blog is meant to be an independent source of information and should be viewed as an impartial source of information.
5. The conversational tone is different. If the company website is formal and the blog is relaxed and informal.

There will generally be one overriding reason which will dominate all of the others. If search engine placements are the most important reason, then we recommend separating the blog and website because the power of linking from an external source is so powerful.

Chapter 10 How to Use Your New Blog

WordPress is an Open Source product which means there are hundreds of developers worldwide working on developments, plug-ins and improvements and it is free. WordPress is available in hosted and self-hosted versions. For business blogging, we recommend the self-hosted version.

The blogs we produce for our clients are powered by WordPress. Although they may take a little longer to configure than other blogs, they are completely customizable. It is currently our top choice for business blogging.

The Blogging Plan

Think of a blogging plan as a roadmap. Use your blogging plan to create focus and purpose for your blog. This can be a simple one page document, but it helps you develop your vision and reason for blogging.

What is My Purpose for Blogging?
For business blog marketing, purposes can include any of the following:
1. Reach new customers or markets
2. Promote products
3. Visibility and branding
4. Search engine rankings
5. Be recognized as an authority
6. Communications

Who is Your Audience?
Many times this is the same as your customer. This includes things like age, income, gender, etc. Are they home owners? What are their interests? Use this kind on information to select

topics and how you communicate your ideas.

What will you write about?
Remember that your postings should be interesting to your
audience and relevant to your business. Choose topics that you
have an interest and passion for. This way your enthusiasm will
show and you will enjoy it more.

Keyword Plan
If one of your purposes is to promote your company website on
the search engines, then choose keyword phrases that are relevant
to your topic(s). Develop specific pages each phrase will link to.

Developing a Blogging Schedule
Blog a minimum of three times a week if you want to develop an
audience and get good results with the search engines. It's easiest
if you set aside some time either every day or every other day at
the same time.

Remember to relax, have fun and enjoy. Writing can be fun, even
therapeutic. It can be exciting when you start engaging others in
conversations.

Overview and Features

Your new WordPress blog has been installed and then configured
for maximum search engine compatibility. A few of your blogs
specially added features include:

1. **Permalinks:** For each blog entry a permanent URL is set-
   up and remains unchanged unless removed by you. A blog
   entry will move down the front page and then eventually
   off of it.

2. **SiteMap Generator:** Generates an XML sitemap for easy spidering by search engines.
3. **Feedburner:** Provides custom RSS feeds and management tools.
4. **Google Analytics:** Website visitor traffic statistics has been added to your blog. You will need a Google email account (Gmail) to access this.
5. **Akismet:** Monitors incoming comments and automatically removes Spam comments.

Login

Login to your new blog by clicking on the login link on your blog and then using your user name and password.

Admin Panel

Your admin panel is broken up into several major categories:

1. **Dashboard:** This shows an overview of all activity including postings, comments and incoming links.
2. **Write:** This is where you prepare your postings, choose categories, add photos and images. There are two views: Visual and Code.
3. **Manage:** This is the main management area. You can select existing entries to delete or edit. You can manage postings, auxiliary site pages and categories from here.
4. **Comments:** This is where you can moderate, edit, view or delete comments. You can view comments that have been tagged as Spam.
5. **Blogroll:** Here you add links to sites that you visit often and share them on your blog.
6. **Users:** Add, edit or delete users and assign security rights. Update passwords here.
7. **Presentation, Plugins and Options:** These are the areas where we set-up and configured your blog for you.

Adding and Managing Categories

Categories represent a summary of content that can be found on your entire blog. Categories give your blog focus and act as an ongoing reminder of your blogging plan. They are important to the search engines since these names are link anchor text. Clear category titles help direct visitors as they seek information.

Category Title
The category title should be directly related to the subject matter and serve many purposes. Blog categories will…
1. Define your blog's purpose and content
2. Keeps you on topic in writing blog posts
3. Act as a table of contents for your blog
4. Create related grouping of content
5. Makes it easier for readers to find related postings (user friendly)
6. Using keywords in category names make your blog SEO friendly

In business blog marketing, search engine rankings are extremely important. Using keywords in the category names is given a very high importance with the search engines and these appear on every page within your blog.

How many categories should you have? Five or six is a good number. Too few really organize your postings and too many and it becomes too confusing to visitors.

Categories if used correctly organize your blog and make it easier for both the writer and visitor.

Add / Manage Categories
Adding new categories is easy in your new blog. You can add a

category while you are writing a new post. There is a place to add just above the listing of categories on the right side.

You can also add, edit or delete categories by going to:

Manage>> Categories from your admin panel.

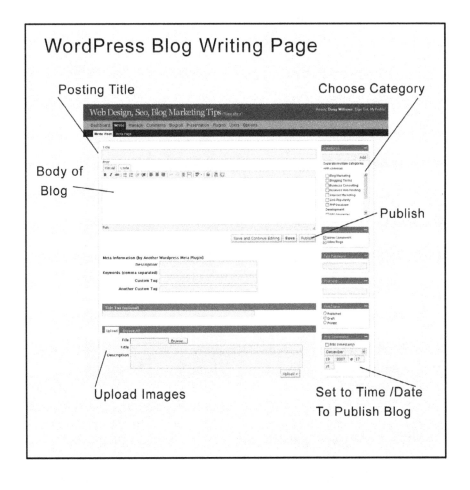

How to Write a Blog Post

Writing and publishing posts in your new blog is very simple and straight forward. The blogs we prefer are powered by WordPress.

To write a blog entry:
1. Login to your Blog Administration Panel.
2. Click the tab for Write.
3. Start filling in the blanks.
4. When you are ready, click Publish.

Yes this <u>is</u> simple. Here are more details about the features you will find in the "Write" area.

Your Drafts: Drafts are posts that are saved and not yet published. Click on the title link of any draft to continue editing. Click on Publish when you are ready to post to your blog and to the World.

Title: This is where you enter the title of your post. Avoid using the same title twice as that will cause problems. You can use commas, apostrophes, quotes, hyphens/dashes, and other typical symbols.

Post: This is where you create the body of your posting. There are two modes: Visual and Code. Visual works like a word processor with formatting buttons just above the text box. These buttons produce HTML tags for bold, italic, image, link, lists, and more. Code allows editing of the HTML code. Just below you will find Save and Continue Editing, Save and Publish.

Tip- You can write a post in Word or other word processor but always paste the content into NotePad or save as plain text. Pasting formatted text directly into your posting area will bring along unwanted formatting and cause unexpected font and text problems. These can only be fixed in the code view.

Categories: This is the list of categories for your site. Check the categories the post belongs to and uncheck the default if it does not apply.

More WordPress Features
Custom Fields offer a way to add information to your site. Custom Fields can modify the way a post is displayed. These are primarily used by plugins, but you can manually edit that information in this section.

Discussion: There are two checkboxes that normally should be left checked. Allowing comments allows visitors to submit comments. Allowing Pings allows pingbacks or trackbacks to this particular post.

Excerpt: An Excerpt is a summary or brief teaser of your posts featured on the front page of your site. If you want to have a summary of the post show, rather than the first paragraph or so, write the summary of your post in the excerpt field.

Meta Information: This is an SEO feature. Add a one sentence description of your post using keywords if possible. List keywords used, each separated by a comma. These will be added to the META Tags of your post.

Post Author: This is where the author of the post's name is chosen from a pull down list. Authors are added to your site by registering and through USERS >>Users and Authors panel.

Post Password: To keep this particular post private so that only those with the password can read it, enter a password here.

Post Slug: This will "clean up" your post title to create a link.

The commas, quotes, apostrophes, and other non-HTML favorable characters are changed and a dash is put between each word.

Post Status: Shows the current status of your post: Draft, Published or Private. Status can be changed here.

Timestamp: By default, at the time the post is saved, that will be the date and time of the post within the database. To change this, click the checkbox and change the date and time information. All posts dated in the future will not appear on the site until that time has passed. If you wish to write posts that will automatically appear on your schedule, set the date and time here.

Trackbacks: Trackbacks let other blogs know you've referenced one of their articles. To send trackbacks from this post, enter the URL or website addresses in the box, separating each one by a space.

Upload /Browse: Allows Images to be added to a post. Upload takes the image from your computer. Browse allows use of images already uploaded.

Acknowledgement: These instructions are summarized from the WordPress website:
(http://codex.wordpress.org/Writing_Posts)

Write Now and Post Later

WordPress blogs have a feature called Post Timestamp. This allows you to write blog postings in advance and then publish them according to your schedule.

I use this for 90% of my blog postings. I write 1-2 articles per day and pick out the ones I want for my blog which is published every other day. Sometimes I will write 3-4 consecutive pieces that I want to post and I schedule them using Timestamp.

Let's say you have a three times per week posting schedule and you are getting ready to go on vacation. You could let your blog sit idle for that week or two, or you can write your topics ahead of time and then schedule them.

How it works: By default, Timestamp uses the current date and time for each posting. You can write your topics ahead of time and then edit the Timestamp to the date and time you want each posting to appear. When you are finished writing, click on "Publish" and your posting is saved and will appear on your blog exactly at that day and time.

Productivity Tool: Let's say you are a business owner and you have a demanding and busy schedule. You can block out a morning once a week to spend on writing. You can still publish three times per week by writing all three posts at one time and editing the Timestamp for each posting.

Improve Quality: Write your posting in advance and then schedule your posting with Timestamp. You can still go in and edit your posting, links, trackbacks, insert any pictures, etc. Just save it after editing.

Post Slug

WordPress will "clean up" your post title to create a link. The commas, quotes, apostrophes, and other non-HTML favorable characters are changed and a dash is put between each word. This title gets converted into a permanent page name automatically by your blog. Use the Post Slug feature to create a different page name.

The Post Slug is located in the right sidebar in your blog writing area. If the section isn't open, click the plus symbol to expand it. Post Slug is a manual override to this automatic page naming.

Why Important
Now why is this important? If you used a very long title such as "Marketing Plan Ideas for Small Business Owners" the page URL would automatically become "/marketing-plan-ideas-for-small-business-owners.php." Using Post Slug, you could enter "Marketing Plan Ideas" and the new page URL would become "/marketing-plan-ideas.php."

Search engines will penalize blog postings with over length page titles. They do this because of spammers who use long page names stuffed with keyword phrases. Page names are very important to the search engines for SEO. Post Slug allows you to control page names.

Using this same example, let's say a very important keyword phrase for you was "marketing planning." You can use Post Slug to shorten and name the page with your keyword phrase.

You don't have to use this Post Slug feature and WordPress will automatically remove punctuation and create page names out of your blog titles. Post Slug does give you control of the permanent page name.

Adding Images to Your posting

Make your postings interesting using graphics and images. You can add all types of images to your blog. People pay attention to graphics. Graphic images tell stories, provide guidance, and help your reader understand what you are writing about. Add charts, screen shots, graphs or photos. Creating visuals tells the story better and faster than words alone.

How to upload

1. From the write tab start a posting. While in the visual mode, click where you want to add the image. (If you have previously saved your post, you will be in the manage area under posts).
2. On the Upload Image panel, click Upload.
3. Click Browse and select the image file and click Open.
4. Add a title describing the image (optional).
5. Click Upload.
6. Choose either thumbnail or full size. Then choose Link To: None. We will add the link later if you want.
7. Click send to editor. This moves the image to the post editor.
8. To get the text to wrap around the image and move the image to one side we will use the Align command.
9. Switch to code view and locate the image. Add either align="right" or align="left" just before the ALT. Here is an example: <img src="http...newphoto.thumbnail.jpg" align="right" alt="new photo" />
10. In Visual mode you can click on the image and link it to a webpage if you wish.

Graphics need to be in a web compatible format such as JPG or GIF.

Tip: If your images exceed 450 pixels in size use a thumbnail to automatically resize the image to something that fits into your blog posting. You may also use your favorite graphics program to resize images.

Creating Video Blogs

Adding video is easy to do and adds a new dimension to your blog postings. Video spices up your postings and gives your audience a chance to meet the author and gain insights beyond what was already presented in the text.

Video clips added into your blog are a good marketing tool to increase customer communication, add a more personal image to your message and increase your web presence. Search engines now have video search capabilities. I have heard it said that if a picture is worth a thousand words, then a video is worth a million.

Adding a Video
This process requires that you post your video first on a website such as YouTube.com or Veoh.com. You will then embed the video into your blog posting. You can also add interesting videos from other sources into your posting (many sources allow this). Adding videos cannot be done using the Visual editor, so it requires going into your user profile, turning off the visual mode, adding the video code and then re-enabling visual mode.

Here is the step by step process.

1. Write your posting as you normally would and save it as a draft
2. Go to your user profile. Users>>Your Profile
3. Uncheck the box at the top "Use the visual editor when writing"
4. Update your profile
5. Return to your posting
6. Add the "Embed Code" from a video hosting website
7. Save your posting
8. Return to your user profile and re-enable the visual editor

Example: <object ...... /object>   see below

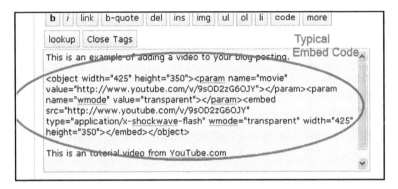

Managing Blog Comments

Comments provide a wonderful degree of interactivity with many obvious benefits. Blogging is supposed to be a two-way conversation; blogging without comments feels like you are talking with a brick wall. With comments you get feedback, questions, interesting ideas and carefully crafted responses. Unfortunately, you will also get Spam and nonsense comments.

Comment Spam

Ideally the blogosphere would be free of solicitations for drugs to enlarge your manhood, or drug pedaling bots wanting you to buy from their online pharmacy. But for these, we have installed Akismet on your Blog. Akismet is a program that combats comment spam.

Akismet checks suspicious comments submitted on your site against a database of recognized and known spam. These are reported through other bloggers, forums, wikis, and contact forms. If Akismet catches a comment, it's probably spam.

Comment Management
You can manage your comments by logging into your Admin Panel >> Comments. Under comments there are three categories.

Comments: You can view, edit or delete past comments

Awaiting Moderation: Here you can approve or delete pending comments

Akismet Spam: These are comments marked as Spam. These can be deleted or marked as "Not Spam"

By moderating your blog comments, you can control which comments appear publicly on your blog. As you write and post each blog, you can control whether anyone can comment on your blog entries by un-checking the box under "Discussion" that says "Allow Comments".

You may also set a number of comment options by going to the Admin Panel >> Options >> Discussion to configure how you want to handle comments.

Building Visitor Traffic

Is what you write worthy of being read by millions? The bottom line is that nothing builds a following of regular readers than adding new, fresh and regular content. You need to take every opportunity to provide a good user experience.

Content is Supreme
When you focus on writing postings of real value instead of churning out disposable text, your readers will notice. They will refer others to your site.

What kinds of topics work? What do prospects want to know about? Can you supply news or latest statistics? Use frequently asked questions from phone calls and emails as ideas for topics to write about. Use press releases, case studies, product reviews and testimonials.

People are searching for specific information about a specific solution. These are more likely to come up on search engine inquiries.

Visit Other Blogs

It is important to become involved with the blogging community. You must be an active participant to generate traffic. Visit blogs and forums. Spread the word about your blog and it will certainly attract readers.

Find blogs dealing with your subject and comment on their postings. Commenting on other blogs will leave trackbacks and will encourage others to click thru to your site. When you engage in dialogue, your visibility will increase

Linking is important

Incoming links is important to search engine visibility. You must give in order to receive. Link to blogs and websites that support what you are saying. Find good statistics, lists and trend information and link to it.

Tip: If you publish good statistics, lists and trend information, others will link to you.

Measuring Your Blogging Results

Are you getting results? You may need to adjust your topics or

188

your writing style. You will find some postings are wildly successful and others are ignored. The strategy is simple; figure out what is working… and do more of it.

Website Statistics: This is the first indicator to show improvement. We have installed Google Analytics on your new blog and you will need a Google email (Gmail) account to view your results. You will be able to track the number of visitors that visit; which pages they view; average time spent; the numbers of pages viewed and much more.

SEO Metrics: Monitor the website statistics for growth and change. In addition, measure the numbers of inbound links, and keyword rankings on the search engines.

Blogging Metrics: Blogging has its own set of metrics to track. Check your blog Dashboard for these in your admin area. These include the number of comments you receive, the number of inbound links to your blog postings and Trackbacks (these are link backs from blogs) submitted. You know you are making impact when others link to your postings.

Business Measurements: This is the important bottom line and usually the slowest place to see results. Are your blog postings generating inquiries and sales leads, improving conversions or increasing the size of your average sale?

After setting your metrics and looking at your statistics, you can then compare the results to other forms of marketing communications you use to promote your business.

"Drive thy business, let not that drive thee." – Benjamin Franklin

"People don't want to be marketed to; they want to be communicated with." -- Flint McGlaughlin

Glossary: Terms Bloggers Use

As with any new technology, blogging has its own jargon. These are some of the words and definitions of blogging.

Adbrite – An advertising program that allows website owners to generate income from visitor traffic. A keyword driven marketplace for buying and selling advertising space on individual websites.

Adsense –Google advertising program that allows website and blog owners to generate income from displaying relevant Google ads on their websites.

Aggregator – Software or web program that gathers syndicated web content such as news headlines, blogs, podcasts, and vlogs in a single location for easy viewing. Also known as a feed aggregator, RSS Aggregator or a feed reader.

Ajax - Acronym for Asynchronous JavaScript and XML. A combination of several programming tools to build interactive applications. Allows the content of a web page to be updated or changed without the entire page being reloaded.

Anonoblog - a blog run by an anonymous author(s). The blog may display some information about the author(s), but not reveal the author's true identity.

Atom – (Atom Publishing Protocol) A specific web feed format that uses an XML language and is a simple HTTP-based protocol for creating and updating Web resources.

Audioblog - A blog that mainly publishes audio files (music or podcasting) sometimes with text and keywords for search engine optimization.

Audioblogging – The act of using audio to reach the audience instead of text used by traditional blogs.

Autocasting – Automated form of podcasting that uses software to convert text from RSS feeds into audio formats.

b5media – Commercial blogging network with more than 250 blogs. In a commercial blog network the organization owns the blogs and hires writers to create blog postings.

Biblioblogosphere - The community of library and librarian blogs is known as the biblioblogosphere.

Blaudience – Short for Blog Audience. A blaudience is the audience or readers of a blog.

Blawg – Commonly called lawyer blogs. These are generally by lawyers, law students or law professors and focus on commentary about the law.

Bleg – To use a blog to beg for assistance. This can be for information or money. Someone who "blegs" is called a "blegger."

Blistless or B-listless - When a blogger loses interest and becomes listless or apathetic about posting. See Blogathy.

Blog – Short for "Web log." A web application that contains periodic postings on a webpage. These are often but don't have to be in reverse chronological order.

Blog carnival – A type of blog event. Similar to a magazine that is dedicated to a single event or topic. Readers are asked to submit articles for inclusion in the upcoming event.

Blog client – Blogging software which manages (posting, editing) for blogs.

Blog farm – A set of blogs that are interlinked to form a blog network.

Blog feed – XML Machine-readable versions of the blog that may be "syndicated" for further distribution on the web. These are generated by the blogging software in formats such as RSS and Atom.

Blog fodder – Interesting ideas that can be used as material for your next blog posting.

Blog hopping – Following links from one blog entry to the next and along the way reading and leaving comments.

Blog mute - Someone who seldom puts up a blog posting.

Blog site – Short for blog website. A blog is short for weblog and is a user generated website that allows for postings that are listed in reverse chronological order.

Blogads – Ads specifically for blogs that allow blog owners to earn advertising income.

Blogathy – Short for blog + apathy. This is someone that does not care about posting today.

Blogcasting – Combining podcasting and blogging into a single website.

Blogger – The author of a blog. One who keeps and or writes a blog.

Blogger – A free blog publishing system owned by Google. Blogs can be hosted on the blogspot.com (Google's Server) or externally on the user's own server.

Bloggernacle – Short for "blog" and "Tabernacle". Blogs written by and for Mormons.

Bloggies – Blog awards that were started in 2001. Bloggies are an annual blog awards that involve nominations and then chosen by the public.

Blogging platform – This refers to the blogging software which is used to create the blog. Popular blogging platforms include WordPress, Blogger, TypePad and Movable Type.

Blogging -The act of writing and posting a blog.

Blogins - Short for "blog" and "login." This is a list of a list of blog logins or passwords.

Blogiverse - see blogosphere.

Bloglet - A small blog entry, usually one or two sentences long. Also a discontinued service that allowed visitors to subscribe to email versions of your post.

Bloglines – A web based news aggregator. Free online service that allows searching, subscribing, creating and sharing news feeds and blog feeds.

Blogoneer – Short for blog + pioneer. This is a person who blogs with an expert or pioneering attitude.

Blogopotamus – A very long blog posting.

Blogorrhea – An unusually high volume of blog postings. Frequently refers to meaningless ranting and raving on a blog.

Blogosphere - All blogs that make up the Internet blogging community. Also called blogistan, blogspace or blogiverse.

Blogroll – A listing of favorite blogs and websites usually in the sidebar of a blog. Also referred to as link lists or bookmarks.

Blogsnob – A blogger who refuses to respond to comments from people outside of their circle of friends.

Blogspot – Free blog hosting service for Blogger.

Blogstorm – When a large amount of blogging controversy, discussion, information and opinion erupts around a particular subject. Sometimes called a blogswarm.

BlogThis – Pioneered by Blogger.com. Allows the reader to generate a blog entry based on the blog entry he/she is reading, and post to their blog from their browser toolbar.

Bloll – Short for blog troll. A Bloll is a commenter whose sole purpose is to attack the views expressed on a blog and incite a flamewar. See Troll.

Blooger – Short for blog + booger. This is a blogger who lacks good manners and acts in an immature adolescent way.

Blook - This is a shortening of "looks like a book" and is a book created from a blog. Typically published in a serialized form one chapter at a time.

Blurker – Someone who visits and reads many blogs but never leaves any trace such as comments or any contribution to a discussion.

Boreblogging - Writing about personal matters that are barely interesting even to the writer.

Catblog – A blog about cats and posting pictures of cats. "Friday catblogging" has become the traditional day for people to post pictures of cats on their blogs.

Categories – A method of organizing blog content into logical groupings. Categories represent a summary or list of content that can be found on your entire blog.

Celeblog – A blog written about or by a celebrity. Usually focuses on news, gossip and often contains embarrassing or revealing paparazzi photos.

CEOBlog – A blog maintained by a chief executive officer of a company.

CGI-BIN–A place (folder) where common gateway interface (CGI) scripts are stored for a website or blog.

Clog – A shortened form of Corporate Blog. This is a blog published and used by a company or corporation to reach its organizational goals.

CMS - Short for Content management system. Software that allows website or blog users to login and update content online. The content is usually stored in a database and the web page or blog page is created dynamically.

Collaborative blog – A blog written by multiple people and based on a single unifying theme. Also known as a group blog.

Comment spam – Unwanted comments that attempt to drive visitors to another blog site. Usually generated by automatic software or "spambots." This is a serious problem that requires anti comment spam software on most blogs. Similar to email spam.

Commenter – Someone who participates in a blog discussion and leaves remarks / comments.

Comments – Comments are submitted by readers of blogs enabling them to leave remarks and add to the "blog conversation." These usually appear at the bottom of a blog posting.

Creative Commons – A non-profit organization. Creative Commons has developed a set of free public licenses to enable authors to share their work with others. See Some Rights Reserved.

Crisis blog – A blog created to deal with natural disasters such as Katrina and the Indonesian tsunami. Also refers to a blog dealing with a public relations crisis for an organization.

CSS– Cascading Style Sheets are a standard for specifying the appearance of text and other webpage elements.

Dark blog -A non-public blog (e.g. behind a firewall). This usually uses a desktop blogging client or an off-line blog management tool.

Dashboard – The primary screen visible when you login to your blogging account. This summarizes the current status and shows the controls for operating your blog.

Del.icio.us – Social bookmarking web service for storing, sharing web bookmarks. Announced in September 2007, the website's name is planned to change to "Delicious" when the site redesign is released.

Digg – Social bookmarking site. News stories, blog postings and websites are submitted by users. The most popular are promoted to the front page of Digg.com.

Digged – Digged means to have a link placed on digg.com and can drive traffic to your blog. Digg is a user driven social content website. All of the content on Digg is submitted by their community of users.

Dooced – To be fired because of comments made by an employee on a personal blog.

Down thread – Earlier blog postings or comments that are found below the post.

Edublog – An education related blog. This can include blogs written for or by teachers. They can be used for educational policy or classroom assignments.

Event blog - A blog that is focused and contains content specific to an event.

Expandable post summaries – The first paragraph or two appears on the index or home page of the blog with a link to the full article.

Feedblitz – A service that monitors blog and RSS feed updates and turns these into emails for subscribers.

Feedburner – A Google owned feed management provider that provides services for blogs and RSS feeds. They offer tracking the statistics RSS feed usage.

Fisking - To rebut a blog entry in a detailed point-by-point criticism that highlights perceived errors.

Flame - An intentionally crude or abusive remark, usually of a personal nature.

Flamewar – An electronic insult match with repeated abusive and insulting email or blog exchanges.

Flickr – A digital photo management and sharing website. Flickr allows photos to be tagged and browsed by folksonomic means.

Flog – Short for Fake Blog. This is a ghostwritten blog written as a marketing tool. Similar to astroturfing (fake grass roots campaign).

Folksonomy – Short for folk (or folks) and taxonomy. A user generated taxonomy used to categorize and retrieve Web pages, photographs, Web links and other web content using open ended labels called tags.

Footer – The bottom part of a blog or webpage. Usually consists of navigation links and a copyright statement.

FTP - Short for file transfer protocol. A standard protocol for exchange of files between computers on the Internet.

Group blog- A blog with more than one regular contributing writer. Also known as a Collaborative blog.

Gulog – A shortened version of gulag and blog. This is used to describe a blog that is so dismal and depressing; it's as if it were written in a Soviet labor camp.

Header – The topmost portion of a web page or blog page. Common elements include website title, graphics and navigation.

HTML – Acronym for Hyper Text Markup Language. The dominant programming language used to create websites and web pages on the World Wide Web.

Icerocket – Search engine specialized in searching blogs, also searches web and MySpace.

Index page – The home page or front page of a blog or website. This is the default page that displays when the top level of a website is accessed.

K-log – A knowledge focused blog that is posted on a company intranet for sharing company knowledge.

Linguablog - A blog about linguistics, translation, languages, or other language-related subjects.

Link love – Posting a link to sites that you enjoy, admire, or find useful. Frequently these are credible and reputable resource sites.

Link popularity – A measurement of the quality and quantity of inbound links to a webpage. A factor which affects a website's search engine rankings.

Linkbaiting – Content on a website or blog that is designed for the specific intention of gathering links from as many different sources as possible.

Live Bookmarks – A feature of the Firefox web browser. Updated content from your favorite sites is brought to you.

LiveJournal – A free blog publishing system owned by SixApart. In addition to being a blogging platform, LJ is a virtual community with some social networking features.

Mashup –A web application that combines data from multiple sources into a single integrated tool. Example: Cartographic data from Google Maps is used to add location maps in a real estate listings website.

Medblog - A blog that deals with health and medicine.

Metablog – This is a blog about blogging.

MicroBlog – A blog that allows up to 140 character long posts. Twitter is the most popular and allows text messaging for blog postings via cell phone.

Milblog – A War Blog or Military Blog is a blog about the military or covering news events concerning an ongoing war.

Moblog – This is short for mobile blog. A blog that features posts from a mobile phone. These are often photoblogs.

Movable Type – A blog publishing platform developed by California based Six Apart in 2001. Movable Type needs to be installed on a user's own web server.

Movlogs – These are mobile video blogs. These are similar to a Moblog, but they feature videos.

Multi-blog –To create or maintain multiple blogs at the same time with a single installation of the Blogging software.

Multi-blogger - An individual or business that runs multiple blogs.

Navbar – Short for navigation bar. A common navigation feature, this is a horizontal row of navigation buttons or links usually located near the top of a website or blog.

Newsgator – A News Aggregator service that displays content news and updates from the Web, the blogosphere.

Odeo – Online application that allows recording and sharing of podcasts.

OPML – Short for Outline Processor Markup Language. This is an XML format that allows exchange of outline-structured information.

O'Reilly Media – Company that originally coined the term "Web 2.0" in 2003. Company was established by Tim O'Reilly in 1978. In 1992 they published the first book about the Web.

PageRank – Google's measurement of how important a page is and affects search rankings. This is an index that values Web pages on a scale of 0 to 10, based largely on link popularity.

Pageflakes – Ajax-based start page similar to iGoogle. Allows users to read news and blogs, check their email, etc.

Permalink –Short for permanent link. For a blog entry, it is a unique URL that remains for the life of a blog.

Phlog – Similar to a blog, but runs off a Gopher protocol server. These are typically hosted off home servers running some sort of UNIX operating system.

Photoblog – A blog whose primary content is photos. The emphasis is on the photography, not just images that explain or illustrate the text.

PHP – Short for Hypertext Preprocessor. An open source, server-side HTML scripting language used to create dynamic Web pages.

A programming language for creating web applications.

Ping – Short for Packet Internet Groper. A utility that forwards data packets to notify or verify a connection. Helps to notify blog tracking tools for updates, changes and trackbacks.

Pingback - See TrackBack.

Pingoat – A web service that notifies dozens of blog ping servers every time you make a new post or update your blog. Similar to Pingomatic.

Pingomatic – Service used by most blogs to notify other ping servers every time you post a new article on your blog. They relay your ping to over 15 other ping engines.

Placeblog – A blog that focuses on the events and people of a local area. Place Blogging has a "hyperlocal" scope.

Plugins – A computer program that works with a software application to provide a specific function. WordPress plugins can add specific features to expand a blogs functions.

Podcasting – Originally short for "iPod broadcasting" but now means posting audio and video material on a blog and its RSS feed, for playback on mobile devices and personal computers.

Political blog –A blog that comments on politics. Political blogs often have a clearly stated political bias.

Post entry- A single or individual blog article of any length and can be made up of text, graphics or video. Collectively, blog postings make up a blog.

Problogger – This is a professional blogger who gets paid to blog.

Progblog - A progressive blog that supports left, liberal or green political ideologies.

Project blog – A blog dedicated to a specific project. This can range from a hobby project to a larger corporate project.

Public voice - The collective voice of individual consumers over the Internet, often influencing consumer behavior.

Radio Userland – One of the early Blog publishing platforms that is still in use today. This was the first blogging software to allow adding audio which later became podcasting.

Read-Write Web – Another name for Web 2.0. The second generation of the web, making collaboration and interacting easier using blogs and wikis.

Reciprocal links – These are links to another website placed on your site in exchange for links back to your site from theirs. Used to improve search engine rankings. Sometimes called link love.

RSS aggregator – See Aggregator.

RSS feed – See Web Feed.

RSS –Really Simple Syndication. A family of web feed formats used in web syndication. These are an XML based system for aggregating information from blogs, news and frequently updated websites.

Scribosphere – The community of blogs written and maintained by screenwriters and aspiring screenwriters.

Semantic Web – The future evolution of the World Wide Web. The Semantic Web will allow people to more easily find, share, and combine information.

SEO – Short for search engine optimization. Techniques and strategies (white hat, black hat) to gain higher rankings in the search engine results.

Shocklog – These are blogs that use slander to sling mud at current affairs, public individuals, institutions and so on. Originated in The Netherlands.

Sidebar – Columns on one or both sides of the main body area in a blog or website. In blogs, a sidebar will frequently contain blogroll links, categories, contact information etc.

Sideblog – A smaller blog placed within the sidebar of a blog. This blog within a blog is used as an easy way to list out interesting links. Sometimes called a link blog.

Skins - Customized or interchangeable graphic templates for blogs or websites. Altering the graphic look is sometimes called skinning the blog.

Social networking – Social networking is linking people to each other in some way. Social networking sites bring people together who are interested in a particular subject.

Some rights reserved – This is a concept started by Creative Commons without any charge. This allows copyright holders to more easily share a copyrighted work and overcome the inherently restrictive nature of copyright law.

Sphere – Blog search engine based on algorithms that combine semantic matching with authority factors.

Splog –Short for Spam Blog. This is a blog which is intentionally fake and doesn't add any written value. Used to increase Page Rank or get ad impressions.

Storyblog – Blogs used to publish stories, poetry and other creative writing; usually by aspiring writers.

Tag cloud – A graphical view of keywords used on a website or blog. Tags are typically listed alphabetically, and tag frequency is shown with font size or color.

Tags – Keywords/phrases that describe the content of a web site, bookmark, photo or blog post.

Tech blog – A blog that focuses on new technology information.

Technorati – Blog search engine that competes with Google, Yahoo, Sphere and IceRocket.

Template – Pre-designed blog or website formats for text and graphics.

TrackBack – Alerts a web or blog author that somebody has linked to one of their documents. This allows writers to keep track of who is linking to their blog postings or web content.

Troll – Someone with the extreme opposite view of the theme of the blog who comments in order to attack the views expressed. See Bloll.

Typepad – Paid hosted blogging platform from Six Apart. Originally launched in 2003, TypePad was based on the Movable Type blogging platform.

URL – Uniform Resource Locator. The complete address for a webpage or file. Example: http://www.dougwilliams.com/index.php

Vlog –Short for video blog. This is a blog that mainly publishes videos. Video podcasting is sometimes called vodcasting.

Vlogging – Short for Video Blogging. Posting blogs that primarily feature video instead of text.

Vorage – The act of foraging for video to use in Vlogging.

Web 2.0 – A term coined by O'Reilly Media in 2004 to describe a second generation of the web. This describes more user participation, social interaction and collaboration with the use of blogs, wikis, social networking and folksonomies.

Web feed – These allow subscribers to see new content as they are published on blogs and websites. Sometimes called an RSS Feed.

Web Syndication – A form of syndication in which a section of a website is made available for other sites to use. Examples are RSS and Atom feeds.

Weblog Awards –Annual blog awards program, considered the largest of the annual blog award competitions.

Weblog - An online journal or diary on a specific subject. Also referred to as a blog.

Widgets – Visual objects, icons or graphical interface elements that can be manipulated by the computer user to perform a desired function online or on their computer.

Wiki – Short for "wiki wiki" which means "rapidly" in the Hawaiian language. Wiki is a website that allows visitors to edit content using their browser. This is a collaborative website.

Wordpress.com – Free blogging platform, this is the hosted version of the WordPress blog. Competes with Blogger and Typepad.

Wordpress.org – Most popular self-hosted blogging platform. Open source, written in PHP and completely customizable.

XML - Short for eXtensible Markup Language. A simple, very flexible text format derived from SGML; a general-purpose markup language for blog syndication.

YouTube – Google owned video sharing website where users can upload and share video clips.

Index